Finding
Divine Inspiration

Working With the Holy Spirit in Your Creativity

J. SCOTT McELROY

DESTINY IMAGE® PUBLISHERS, INC.
P.O. Box 310, Shippensburg, PA 17257-0310

"Speaking to the Purposes of God for this Generation and for the Generations to Come."

This book and all other Destiny Image, Revival Press, Mercy Place, Fresh Bread, Destiny Image Fiction, and Treasure House books are available at Christian bookstores and distributors worldwide.

For a U.S. bookstore nearest you, call 1-800-722-6774.
For more information on foreign distributors, call 717-532-3040.
Reach us on the Internet: www.destinyimage.com.

ISBN 10: 0-7684-2702-9
ISBN 13: 978-0-7684-2702-8

For Worldwide Distribution, Printed in the U.S.A.

1 2 3 4 5 6 7 8 9 10 11 / 12 11 10 09 08

DEDICATION

In memory of
Greg Griffen,
friend and mentor and one of the finest men I've known.
Passionate visionary and seeker of souls.
Now joyfully in the arms of his Abba.

For my beautiful family—Danielle, queen of my heart,
Hailee, apple of my eye,
Kaia, my son of promise,
and Ellie, the best dog ever.

ACKNOWLEDGMENTS

I want to thank my parents, Tom and Carol McElroy, for their encouragement, not only in the writing process of this book, but also in everything I've undertaken in life. They are truly amazing and wonderful examples of faith and perseverance, and without them behind me, I doubt this book would have come about.

My wife, Danielle, has been essential to this writing and publishing process, even though we met several years after it had begun. Her belief in me and in this book is one of the greatest gifts of my life. After the Holy Spirit, she is the key person in the ministry who comes through this message.

My children, Hailee and Kaia, have had their patience stretched while they waited for me to "finish writing." Especially Hailee, who has put up with her dad working on and talking about this book most of her life!

This would not have been possible without the wonderful friends and prayer supporters who have hung in there with me over the years: Becky Roudebush (now Pico!),

Collen Clifford (now Hughes!), Nathan Tobey, Eric and Meredith Poland, Susie and the north-side Renollets, Don and the south-side Renollets, Greg and Karen Griffen, the Carmel Warner and Westfield Warners, the Rolens, Wendy Weeks, the Malloys, the Mathewses, the Gonzaleses, Steven and Amanda Potaczek, Marcia and Keith Calhoun, Dan and Marcia Kiel, Skip Beyer, Scott and Jeanne Rieger, the Wybrows, Joy Herpel, Holly Hintz, Tony Spitler, the Balchs, Amy Mathis, Susan Eudaly, Mylon Miller, , Sarah Fouser, Clark Cassell, Robbie Hunt, the Komasinskis, and the Rays and all the friends and acquaintances that have encouraged this process

Thanks to Ronda Ranalli at Destiny Image for her enthusiasm, coaching, and friendship.

I'm fortunate to be part of Vineyard Community Church in Indianapolis, a place where love flows and the arts are welcomed. Thanks to Randy Gooder and the staff who have prayed for me and affirmed the message of this book. I especially want to thank Randy for his friendship, cheerleading, and help with this manuscript.

Sean Tienhaara's leadership, encouragement, and blessing have opened the doors for so much creative growth in my life. He is connected to many of the personal stories in this book, and his review of this manuscript helped bring it to another level.

Jeff Sparks has been more influential in the development of this book than I think he realizes. He may have been the first person to pray for this message, and he continues to be a faithful prayer supporter. His life and vision for creativity have been an inspiration, and his encouragement and willingness to make introductions has been invaluable.

ENDORSEMENTS

Finding Divine Inspiration is a fresh exploration of the relationship between creativity and the Creator. I was inspired and deeply moved by the personal journey Scott takes us on; I couldn't put the book down! Both practical and insightful—this book is a must-read for any creative spirit in need of encouragement.

Jeff Sparks
President, Heartland Truly Moving Pictures
and the Heartland Film Festival
Founder, The New Harmony Project

This book is a powerful message to everyone involved in the creative arts about how God wants to use *us* to radically impact our generation. It has truly challenged me as a television professional to develop a more listening-to-the-inspiration-of-the-Holy-Spirit lifestyle.

Eric Poland
Emmy Award-Winning Producer

Scott's down-to-earth, practical nature comes through in this witty and insightful book. I love his emphasis on listening to and collaborating with the Holy Spirit. With God's direction and inspiration, the arts can be one of the most powerful tools the Church has for opening hearts to the Spirit's voice. Scott has done an excellent job of leading us into a deeper walk with the Lord that leads to a true collaboration with Him in the arts and the greater drama of life itself.

Dr. Marcus Warner
President, Deeper Walk International
Author, *Toward a Deeper Walk*

CONTENTS

PREFACE

THIS BOOK WAS PUBLISHED almost ten years to the day from when its first thoughts were written onto a floppy disc. It's been an interesting journey from that point to this, characterized by God's incredible faithfulness. He's been faithful to train me in the process of *Finding Divine Inspiration* step-by-step, to bring all the pieces together that make this book possible, and to not give up on me through bouts with discouragement and delay. There is no one like Him!

After a decade of writing about this subject, I'm more excited than ever about the promise of collaborating with the Holy Spirit in the creative process! The signs that God is working in the arts continue to mount, and the opportunities for creativity in the world are exploding.

In the last few years, almost every young person I know has become a creative designer of sorts, building and designing their own Websites at places like MySpace and Facebook.

They take and edit digital photos, develop content, and collaborate endlessly with one another. In another ten years, we'll be living in a very different creative world, enjoying the new freedom and collaboration that new technologies will bring us. As author Daniel Pink says in his introduction to *A Whole New Mind*:

> The last few decades have belonged to a certain kind of person with a certain kind of mind—computer programmers who could crank code, lawyers who could craft contracts, MBAs who could crunch numbers. But the keys to the kingdom are changing hands. The future belongs to a very different kind of person with a very different kind of mind—creators and empathizers, pattern recognizers and meaning makers. These people—artists, inventors, designers, storytellers, caregivers, consolers, big picture thinkers—will now reap society's richest rewards and share its greatest joys.[1]

With the dawn of a new era of creativity worldwide, the timing seems exactly right for the concept of collaborating with the great Creator to be released. Now more than ever, Christian artists have an opportunity to lead the way as we learn to listen to and collaborate with the Holy Spirit.

Though this is not a book about the person of the Holy Spirit, I do mention Him often, and I think it's important to understand a bit about who He is. The Bible tells us that the Holy Spirit is the third person of the Trinity—Father, Son, and Holy Spirit—and that they are all equally and completely one God. This is a mystery that is hard for our finite human minds to grasp.

The Holy Spirit has certain characteristics and functions, including encourager (see Acts 9:31), counselor and teacher (see John 14:26), giver of spiritual gifts (see 1 Cor. 12), source of anointing (see 1 John 2:20,27), giver of inspiration (see 2 Pet. 1:20-21), and teacher (see 1 Cor. 2:13).

Because of these, He is the member of the Trinity often associated with creative endeavors, but we should remember that where He is working, the entire Trinity is present. I say this to make the point that when the term *Holy Spirit* is used in this book, the word *God* also could be substituted.

The subtitle of this book is *Working with the Holy Spirit in Your Creativity*. *Working with* is a broad description that suits a subtitle, but the term I'll use more often in the book is *collaboration*. It's a word that I think accurately captures the essence of our work with God, because He wants us to be fully engaged with Him. It is not a forced cooperation from an overbearing dictator, but an act of joining our will with His, using the talents, abilities, background, and personality that He has given us and discovering the joy of working with Him for His divine, benevolent will.

It *is* such a joy to realize that, though we are all flawed, our perfect God *loves* to partner with us not only to get His message out, but also to help us become everything we were meant to be. I'm still amazed that God has included this flawed vessel in the translation of the *Finding Divine Inspiration* message. It's my hope and prayer that, even with the imperfections in this manuscript and its translator, God will accomplish all that He planned through the concepts in this book.

I look forward to hearing your stories as God brings this to life in you! Please feel free to e-mail me at scott@FindingDivineInspiration.com.

Blessings!

INTRODUCTION

There ain't nothing that can't be done
By me and God
Ain't nobody come in between me and God
One day we'll live together
Where the angels trod
Me and God
We're a team
Me and God
We're a team
Me and God

—Country music singer, Josh Turner, *Me and God*

Ask and it will be given to you; seek and you will find; knock and the door will be opened to you. For everyone who asks receives; he who seeks finds; and to him who knocks, the door will be opened.
                    —Jesus, Matthew 7:7-8

L EARNING TO FIND DIVINE INSPIRATION through working with the Holy Spirit, like so many things in the spiritual life, is very simple, yet very deep. So first I'll say it simply. To learn to work with the Holy Spirit in your creativity, first pursue a relationship with Him. I've included some thoughts on how to do that later in the book. If you are already a Christian, ask Him to reveal and forgive any sins you need to be cleansed of. Then invite Him into your creative process and tell Him you want to partner in what He is doing. Next, listen patiently for anything He wants to say. Finally, get to work, staying sensitive to His guidance.

That's the simple version. If you apply that to your life and creativity, amazing things will happen. Now, let's dig into the deeper truths of *Finding Divine Inspiration*.

CHAPTER 1

A NEW RENAISSANCE

*The true work of art is but a shadow of
divine perfection.*
—Michelangelo Buonarroti

O N A SUNDAY MORNING IN THE WINTER OF 1851, a
writer sat in a church pew in Cincinnati praying
for inspiration. She had been asked to write a fic-
tional story about the evils of slavery in America—a subject
she had become very passionate about—but she had struggled for weeks to find the right words. As she prayed, a vivid
vision suddenly began playing out before her. She saw
scenes of the brutal beating of an old slave and how he for-
gave his murderers and prayed for the salvation of their souls
as he died.

The writer, Harriet Beecher Stowe, rushed home, put
the vision on paper, and submitted it to her editor at the
National Era magazine. The story grew into a series and
then into a book, and its release in 1852 caused a national

sensation. Sales for *Uncle Tom's Cabin* were astronomical, but more importantly, the antislavery sentiment in the North was fully ignited by the riveting story. In fact, it's been said that the book was pivotal in ending slavery in this country. When President Lincoln finally met Stowe during the Civil War, he reportedly said, "So you're the little woman who made the great war."[1]

At a crucial time in history, God used the arts in the form of literary fiction to help change the course of a country. He chose to speak a message through a woman who had never written a book but who prayed and looked to Him for inspiration. The book wasn't perfect, and in fact, it fell into disrepute a century later for racial stereotypes (which were not Stowe's intention), but God powerfully used the writer and her message—flaws and all—to encourage a revolution.

Fast forward to the new millennium. God still is working in the arts to bring change, and He wants to collaborate with you to do it. He wants to lead and inspire you through the Holy Spirit to bring His messages to the world.

There are exciting signs that the Holy Spirit is moving in a new and powerful way, using the media forms that are unique to our age. Millions of people who might not step into a church are being exposed to spiritual truths through artistic expression.

Mainstream music has been invaded by hit songs that feature lyrics about Heaven and a longing for "more." Film has seen an unprecedented increase in well-done, Christ-centered projects like the low-budget movie, *Facing the Giants*, made by an Atlanta church. That movie grossed more than one hundred times its cost and influenced over one thousand people to invite Jesus into their lives. And of course, there was the astounding success of that R-rated film about the crucifixion. It broke through to viewers' hearts and minds in a powerful way *and* broke records at the box office.

Some have said a New Renaissance is coming—a movement to bring Christian spirituality into the arts and the arts back into the Church, a movement that will bring God's messages to the world in uniquely creative ways. I believe this will happen when Christians and Christian artists quit trying to create change through our own power and instead listen to the guidance of the Holy Spirit. Mel Gibson said that he was "just directing traffic"[2] as the Holy Spirit inspired and helped him make *The Passion of the Christ*. James Caviezel, who played Jesus in the film, made a point to take Communion every day during the film's production.[3] A New Renaissance will come when Christian artists actively invite the Holy Spirit into our daily creative process—when we learn to personally collaborate with God.

Collaboration with the Holy Spirit gives our work a depth and authenticity that resonates in the hearts and minds of those who experience it. And it opens avenues in us, the artists, to experience more inspiration and joy in our work. Collaborating with God brings us into the fullness of who we were created to be.

The Arts in Christianity

For too long the Protestant Christian community did not understand the potential of the arts. This lack of understanding probably started during the Reformation, when Protestants rebelled against the Catholic Church's control and turned to the Bible as the highest authority. Along with all of the positive effects of that movement, there was also negative fallout for the arts. When the Reformers discarded most of the Catholic traditions, development of the visual arts was thrown out as well. Many Protestants regarded the arts, with the exception of music, with suspicion, fearing they could encourage idolatry.

Meanwhile, the Catholic Church did continue to sponsor artistic pursuits, but the humanism that became prevalent in the Renaissance slowly replaced faith as art's main influence. For hundreds of years, most Protestants avoided making the visual and dramatic arts a regular part of their tradition, letting those powerful media become the domain of unbelievers instead. The suspicion that the arts were dangerous became a self-fulfilling prophecy when there was little or no Christian influence to temper them. In recent years, we've largely relegated ourselves to lamenting the fact that this powerful form of communication is overwhelmingly under the influence of heathens.

Of course through the years, God has used many Christian artists to make an impact in spite of the Christian culture's neglect of the arts. But so much more is possible. Now is the time for artists to truly seek partnership with God in our work, to experience the journey of true collaboration with the ultimate Creator.

AFFIRMATION FOR A SQUIRMY KID

My own creative journey began in 1969, when I was seven years of age. I had returned to school that August to discover that my teacher was Mrs. Leffle, the prettiest, most modern teacher at Greenbriar Elementary. I soon found out she was also nice. Nice to *me*. In fact, to my delight, Mrs. Leffle took a special interest in me.

She complimented my artwork.

I still have the notes she wrote to my parents detailing my school progress. In one she followed up, "He talks a bit too much and is sometimes restless and squirmy" with, "Scott is most fond of art activities. I enjoy him!" Think that didn't make me want to impress her? A later note said, "Scott's overall citizenship [talking] has improved. I just love his art productions. He certainly has talent!" Talent! I had artistic talent!

That's my first memory of being affirmed as a creative person, and it's had an incredible influence on my life. Whatever happened, I believed I had creative talent—Mrs. Leffle had said it! A few years later, I became a Christian and developed an awareness that God had had a hand in designing me as a creative person. I felt that inherent creativity was something to be proud of, something that made me special, something that I could "use for God" some day.

Unfortunately, over time, my own preconceived notions and pride took me down a path of lip service to God in the surrendering of that creative talent. I felt that if I just did what I desired and prayed for God to bless it, everything would be OK. I thought, *Wasn't He the one who gave all the desires anyway?* I found success as I followed this path, though not usually as much as I wanted, and much of it came after my own scheming or positioning. Rarely did I feel that I knew He had led me in a project or a decision. I thought I probably couldn't know and that the fruit might be seen later.

Thankfully, that is not where I live anymore. Yes, I still get to walk by faith when I don't *feel* God's leading or presence in a project, but I know He is with me because I've invited Him into the process. My creative life has become an exciting partnership with the God who designed me for this purpose.

I've discovered that my Father is interested in me and wills to express Himself through me, and amazingly, more of my true self comes to life when I seek to partner with Him. It's the reality of the biblical concept that, as I give my life to Him, I really find it (see Matt. 10:39).

Our partnership manifests itself in a variety of ways. Sometimes it is in an idea He seems to give or in a check in my spirit to wait or to use or not use a certain element in a project. Often it's just in a nudge to move forward in faith after I've prayed and invited Him into my work, even if I don't sense specific direction. Many times He drops a picture or idea into my head while I'm meditating on Him. As I keep myself open to His voice, He regularly guides me to Scriptures, magazine articles, books, or interactions with people that shed light on the path of my creative process and my life.

The process of entering into this collaboration always begins with and involves prayer and is based on a *listening lifestyle*: living in a way that is focused on hearing the voice of God. Through this process, I often have the true knowledge that He has worked with me. It's a knowledge that brings peace, graciousness in accepting praise or criticism, a wonderful relief from pride, and the freedom to release manipulation and control. If I believe that He has been present and involved, there is less pressure, because He has everything in hand. As I seek Him, He will guide me in the steps that I need to take. This revelation came after a major life crisis: the unexpected end of my marriage, which resulted in a year of laying down nearly all creative expression. Now I am compelled by the Holy Spirit to write about this exciting way of working and living.

INSPIRATION THROUGH COLLABORATION

Outstanding art could be broken down into the elements of talent, skill, and inspiration. We are born with or without talent; it is a gift from God. We develop skill with practice, the one element we have control over. And we look for inspiration from the world around us, from experiences, people, ideas, and God. The Christian artist is especially fortunate, because God our Father can be our overwhelming source of inspiration through His Holy Spirit. He wants to knit together the life we have lived and the things inside of us with His wisdom and insight and to speak truth to someone through the collaborative work. Sometimes it may be a word only for us or sometimes a witness to thousands. It may be designed by Him to impact a specific person or group, or it may end up being a masterpiece.

In *Roaring Lambs*, the late Bob Briner wrote what many of us have thought:

> Christians with direct access to the Creator of the universe and with the indwelling of the Holy Spirit should be and could be the most brilliantly

dazzling artists imaginable and should be and could be creating paintings, sculptures, photographs, and buildings that would draw men and women to the Savior and inspire them to great efforts in building God's kingdom.[4]

The book you are reading is certainly in part about getting closer to that place. But it is more than that. It is about coming into the fullness of life that God has for us, about living life well. We may not achieve the status of being "the most brilliantly dazzling artists imaginable," but by listening for and following God's still, small voice and collaborating with His plans, we'll feel the true success of being sons and daughters who have done our very best and are at peace with the result.

A Change Is Possible

As I mentioned at the beginning of this chapter, many Christians lack understanding of the importance and impact of the arts. With the exception of some of the more liturgical denominations, many of our Protestant churches still are devoid of significant images and artistic works that truly touch the soul.

Through the arts, the Spirit can bypass our intellect and logic and get through to our hearts in a profound way. But because we have often been slow to welcome artistic expressions of faith and slow to use the arts as God intended, the enemy has appropriated them for his own evil purposes. As Briner says, "This is a tragedy, a disaster. Art has not lost its power because of our neglect. Its power is still there, but it's not being used for good."[5]

Another unfortunate reality is that Holy-Spirit-inspired work that profoundly impacts the world—like Stowe's—is not common. Of course, *Uncle Tom's Cabin* was uniquely for that crucial time in history, but we also have been placed in a unique and crucial time. There still are many areas where the salt and light of a witness for God needs to penetrate. The Holy Spirit is changing the trend here, but the impact won't result solely from our educating the church world about the arts or becoming better craftsmen. Results happen as we invite the Spirit to work with us, as we collaborate with Him and yield to Him in our work.

The Church must understand and embrace the arts, and the world must be penetrated with salt and light. These are our dreams and goals. It is the intent of this book to help artists develop the foundation that will make these things possible: listening ears, an obedient heart, a pure mind, and an expectant desire to collaborate with the Creator of the universe. As we let Him have His way, He'll build these things in us.

Second Corinthians 3:2-3 says, "You yourselves are our letter, written on our hearts, known and read by everybody. You show that you are a letter from Christ, the result of our ministry, written not in ink but with the Spirit of the living God...." I believe that the Father wants His creative people to be a living letter in lifestyle, in expression, and in surrender of our creativity to Him, not only generally but also specifically in every project we take on. True collaboration with God is at the foundation of the New Renaissance and the key to finding divine inspiration. If we invite Him into our work, He'll come.

God will renew the arts
by collaborating with you,
His artist.
In that collaboration
you'll experience renewal and
the joy
that you've always wanted.
Start by simply inviting Him
into your creative process
and ask Him to be present
in every part of every project
you work on.

CHAPTER 2

DIVINE COLLABORATION

Whatever God's dream about man may be, it seems certain it cannot come true unless man cooperates.

—Stella Terrill Mann[1]

O NE OF THE FIRST THINGS THAT GOD CHOOSES TO REVEAL about Himself in the Bible is that He is creative. In the first chapter of Genesis, He shows us that He is infinite yet totally focuses on points in time when He will use His creativity to benefit us and Himself. In verse 10, God reveals that He enjoys creativity; it strikes a chord in Him: "And God saw that it was good." Not *good* in the sense of, "Hey, that's pretty good," but "*Yes*! This is right! This is a reflection of Me! I am good in this pure, beautiful way, and I want to share that. This is good like I am good!"

Then in verse 26, God reveals something amazing—a mystery—about His creativity: He chooses to collaborate!

"Then God said, 'Let *us* make man in *our* image, in *our* likeness.'" He seems to be collaborating with the other parts of the Trinity; the Father, Son, and Holy Spirit are working together to create! From that point in time until now, we can see that collaboration is essential for creativity, and it's essential for life.

Adam first experienced collaboration with his Father when "the Lord God took the man and put him in the Garden to work it and take care of it" (Gen. 2:15). It wasn't hard, sweaty work for Adam, like we think of such work today, but a sweet, creative collaboration. The fertile soil parted easily for him. Seeds he planted grew unhindered. Everything he touched was healthy, fruitful, and beautiful. He was fully aware that, though he tended the garden, God made it grow. We may not think much about that today and may even take it for granted, but for Adam this was a daily, demonstrable, exuberant miracle.

In fact, work was a joyous exercise for both God and Adam. It gave a profound sense of usefulness and inclusion to the man as well as joy at the recognition of his Father's creative awesomeness. And God got to experience the exquisite happiness a parent has when a child is reaching his potential of his own free will and enjoying it. The results of this work benefited Adam and (later) his wife with bountiful food and the most beautiful place imaginable to live, but it benefited the Father too. He was fond of taking walks in this garden, enjoying its progress, and savoring its sights and smells, sometimes "in the cool of the day" (Gen. 3:8).

The second record of human and divine collaboration tells of the man and his Father getting together for the exciting task of naming the animals. "He brought them to the man to see what he would name them; and whatever the man called each living creature, that was its name" (Gen. 2:19). What a happy time that must have been! Think of the fun God and Adam were having as God went and picked out a giraffe or a rhino and brought it to his son! Adam might have walked around it, touched it, and listened to the sounds it made while his Father watched with delight and then laughed and applauded at each name.

After the naming of the animals was done, Adam got the opportunity to participate in this creative collaboration at a new level. A part of himself was used to create something totally new: another human being who was wholly different from him, with her own will and life, but at the same time truly a part of him. He loved her, and God loved them, and it was good. The man and his wife began to collaborate together in everything, from work to conversation to sex.

We know what eventually happened, how the man and woman rebelled and everything changed. Though work remained collaboration between man and his Creator, the material the man had to work with became obstinate. Working the soil was now a difficult, sweaty task. Insects and disease attacked his plants. Animals became dangerous. But what was worse was that Adam's relationship with his Father was broken. Where once he lived in tune with God's Spirit, now he was susceptible to the voices of sin, satan, and his own sinful, broken heart.

And that's where we would be stuck today if it were not for the gracious love of God, who through His Son has given us another opportunity to live in tune with His Spirit.

The scientist Francis Bacon said, "Man by the Fall fell at the same time from his state of innocence and from his domain over nature. Both of these losses, however, can even in this life be in some part repaired; the former by religion and faith, and the latter by the arts and sciences."[2]

Although the effects of sin entering into the world were catastrophic, the truth that God designed us to collaborate with Him remains intact. In fact, from the moment of conception, the human experience is a collaborative one. Man and woman both bring indispensable and unique qualities to the union that, with the collaboration of God, will bring forth a new life.

And that's just the beginning. That baby is wired to instinctively collaborate to live. The baby cries; the mother responds. The mother produces milk; the baby sucks. As he grows, the baby will collaborate with others for the rest of his life: in relationships, at school, at work, even in something as passive as watching television—writers and producers and actors could not continue to do what they do without someone to read or watch or hear.

If that child invites God into his life, a profound number of collaborative experiences with God await. The child and God collaborate at the moment of salvation, as the child gives his life to Christ and He takes all his sin. And when the child turns her mind and heart toward reading or hearing the Word, the Holy Spirit will collaborate and bring understanding. If the child leads others to Christ as she grows, she'll collaborate with God by speaking the words the Holy Spirit is guiding her to say. In fact, collaboration is at the core of faith. Faith is the substance of things hoped for, but it can't work without us; it calls for an active hoping on our part. Full participation in faith is not the exercise of personal skill, but the catching of the ball thrown by an eternal partner.[3]

When I first started to walk in the idea of pursuing collaboration with God, I experimented with small details, expecting like a little child that He could guide me in nearly everything. It's important to note that God isn't looking for robot children who never do a thing without His orders, but there are times when He will guide us very specifically.

One day I felt God leading me to take a walk in my parents' neighborhood and sensed He would guide my steps. As I focused on hearing His subtle voice that nudged me along, He led me to turn down one street, walk it for about a mile, and then turn again at an intersection. I asked Him where to go from there and felt Him say to just sit on a low fence by the side of the road. I sat there for maybe a minute when a car came along and hit a tire on the sharp corner of the curb. There was a loud pop from the tire; then it went flat. It was almost a comedic scene as I watched this car slowly roll up and stop directly in front of where I was casually sitting.

An elderly woman got out to see what had happened, and she was surprised when I stood up and offered to help. As I changed the tire for her, I told her about how I'd ended up there at just that moment and talked to her about how much God cares for her. Then I sent her on her way and walked back home, glowing with joy and thanking God for allowing me to collaborate with Him in such a tangible way. When I got back to my parent's house about 20 minutes later, the woman's husband had tracked down our phone number using my last name and had called to tell my mystified mother what had happened.

Through that experience and many others like it, I learned that God loves to collaborate with me for His purposes, especially when I make myself available to Him. And I discovered how fulfilling it can be to trust and obey what He is leading me to do.

CONSCIOUS COLLABORATION

No one, especially a Christian, is excluded from collaborating with our Creator. And as Christians and artists, we have the opportunity to go beyond passive collaboration and to actively seek it. Madeleine L'Engle said, "To co-create with God is our human calling. It is the calling for all of us, His creatures, but it is perhaps more conscious with the artist—or should I say the Christian artist."[4]

The Father longs to collaborate with us, the Christian artists, to draw us into His process and pour His light and joy into it. In the chapters ahead, we'll explore the path that leads to a more natural and consistent experience of that creative collaboration.

God is passionate about collaborating with you.

He can't wait to create beautiful, inspired art with you in true collaboration.

It's what you were made for.

Ask Him what His ideas are, what He wants to do. Then take some time to listen.

CHAPTER 3

THE WORK OF THE ARTIST

*Everything happening, great and small,
is a parable whereby God speaks to us,
and the art of life is to get the message.*
—Malcolm Muggeridge[1]

J UST AS GOD HAS CALLED EVERY PERSON to collaboration, so
He has called us all to listen. We are to listen to ourselves, to each other, to nature, and to the Holy Spirit.
In so doing, we will know Him. Romans 1:19-20 says,
"...what may be known about God is plain to them,
because God has made it plain to them. For since the creation of the world God's invisible qualities—His eternal
power and divine nature—have been clearly seen, being
understood from what has been made, so that men are without excuse." Unfortunately, in our time, most humans don't
know how to consistently listen to or observe and contem-
plate what we see. In fact, we often would rather *not* do
those things.

The rest of that passage in Romans says that this disinterest is part of the price we pay for rejecting the knowledge of God; our thinking has become futile and our foolish hearts are darkened. Just look at the world we have fashioned. It's full of noise and distraction and entertainment. A myriad of flashy, artificial voices compete for attention against the quieter and more authentic voices of God and our true selves. But God, in His great love and mercy, has not given up on getting through. Of course, He has given us the Bible and wonderful preachers and teachers to share the truth in clear ways, but He also has put among us people who share truth in a more subtle, intuitive way. They are people who are wired to listen, who often find that they are unhappy when they tune out the messages and observations that they encounter. These people are the artists, the folks Ezra Pound calls "the antenna of the race." While the rest of society may be tuning out, the artist still is bringing messages from God, even if he doesn't realize it. And he is using his art to make sense of those messages. "Their art is both their tool of discovery and their means of transmitting their findings back to others."[2]

Madeleine L'Engle calls the artist "one still able to see angels,"[3] *angels* meaning those hidden things God is doing in the world that are more easily recognized by children, with their sense of innocence and wonder, than by cynical and hardened adults. Artists may be more apt to embrace mystery, to explore it. And mystery points back to the omnipotence and sovereignty of God.

These messages that artists catch and communicate include all sorts of insights about the nature of the world and the human condition. Very often they get twisted up in the artist's worldview, but even if they are disturbing or sacrilegious, they are still saying something that, if we listen, may ultimately turn us toward God. A song about sex is really expressing a desire to be known by another being, to be fulfilled by intimacy. This is how God designed us, and only He can truly know us and offer unconditional intimacy. (Not that we should make smutty songs a part of our daily diet!) A sacrilegious painting, though heartbreaking, illuminates man's rebellion against God, and the work's hopelessness and emptiness is the very proof that we need more than self-expression to fulfill us.

Nearly all art has the potential to provide some kind of illumination. Imagine the power of art done by Christians who are actively collaborating with the Holy Spirit—art that is infused with inspired, prophetic messages for individuals and cultures. Dallas Willard picked up on the need for this power when he read the writings of the great Christians of the past. He says in *Hearing God*:

> They assured me that the same Spirit who delivered the Scriptures to holy men of old speaks today in the hearts of those who gather around the written word to minister and be ministered to. And they warned me that only if this happened could I avoid being just another more or less clever letter-learned scribe—trying to nourish the souls of my hearers out of the contents of my own brain, giving them only what I was able to work up through my own efforts from the Bible or elsewhere.[4]

There is no reason for Christian artists to continue operating like "clever, letter-learned scribes" lacking inspiration. We can and should expect inspiration and collaboration with the Holy Spirit in our work. If all Christian artists were to really work in this way, while developing their craft to a level of excellence, the glory and personality of God might become unavoidably evident to the world.

WHY ART AFFECTS US

The truth artists get at strikes a chord in us because it speaks to our intuitive side. God designed the arts to jump over our barriers, past our intellect, and to go into our hearts and souls. We connect intuitively with story, sound, and symbol. Plato said, "Music and rhythm find their way into the secret places of the soul."[5] Leanne Payne said, "Reality is…Jesus often taught with stories, and think of all the symbolism in the Bible; Satan as a serpent, the Ark of the Covenant, the cross."[6]

I can think of many times that a work of art, whether visual, musical, or other, has planted a truth deeper in my heart than traditional teaching had been able to. Once, during a series of messages at my church about the prodigal son, one of our artists made several large chalk drawings of scenes from that story, most of them studies of well-known pieces, and hung them on the walls all around the sanctuary. I had been searching for a visual to meditate on when I imagined myself before the Father, but when I saw a black-and-white piece our artist had done of the father greeting the son, it repulsed me. The father seemed too close, too intimate as he held his wayward son's head inches away from his own and looked into his eyes. Over the following weeks, I was continually drawn back to this uncomfortable picture, until at last God broke through to help me understand my position as a son and His intimate love for me. In more than 20 years of being a Christian, no amount of teaching had been able to really bring that home. But that stark chalk drawing did. Now that is the picture I see when I close my eyes and come into my Father's presence. It was a wonderful and life-changing gift.

Of course, the services artists offer our society are endless. In *Imagine*, Steve Turner writes:

The arts can act on God's side by preserving beauty and drawing out the highest achievements capable by humans. The arts can help preserve and renew cultures, and this is a good thing in itself. This must bring God pleasure. The arts can sharpen the vision, quicken the intellect, preserve the memory, activate the conscience, enhance the understanding and refresh the language.

The visual arts help us see with greater clarity. They draw our attention to overlooked details. They restore our sense of amazement. Dance re-sensitizes us to the grace of movement. Fiction provides us with unique access to other minds, cultures and periods of history. Music supplies us with hints of the transcendent. It is surely significant that art suffers when cultures decline. The Old Testament often gives us the haunting image of the cessation of music and singing when a civilization crumbles.[7]

The Way of the Artist

The successful listening artist is one who works from a foundation of contemplation, "seeing, beholding, perceiving some reality," as German Christian philosopher Josef Pieper said. He believed that "the true artist …is not someone who simply… 'sees' things. So that he can create form and image (not only in bronze and stone but through word and speech as well), he must be endowed with the ability to see in an exceptionally intensive manner."[8]

Some mainstream artists (Christian or not) have had an inkling that this ability to see and receive from outside themselves just may be from God. Picasso said, "Something sacred, that's it. It's a word that we should be able to use, but people would take it in the wrong way. You ought to be able to say a painting is as it is, with its capacity to move us, because it is as though it were touched by God."[9] Acclaimed author Kurt Vonnegut Jr. said, "Virtually every writer I know would rather be a musician because music gives pleasure as we never can…. I'm Honorary President of the American Humanist Association, but I simultaneously say that music is the proof of the existence of God."[10] Bono, lead singer of U2, arguably the world's greatest rock band, stated in an interview, "We [U2] have to write songs that raise the temperature of the room and find words for feelings you can't express. And then, as Quincy Jones says, you wait for God to walk through the door. Because in the end, craft isn't enough."[11]

But other artists find it more difficult to acknowledge the influence of the Holy Spirit or God in the creative process. They offer other explanations for the inherent ability to "see." Some follow the thoughts of Plato and Jung: that our seeing is drawn from knowledge we already have that's locked deep inside.[12] Some think it is an expression or perception of the heart; some think artists are like antennae that pick up cosmic signals from the universe; some believe that work calls out to be formed.

Interestingly, many of these thoughts contain an element of truth. We can, in part, draw from that which has been placed in us. Ecclesiastes 3:11 says that God "set eternity in the hearts of men...." As for our hearts speaking, this could also be true. Unfortunately, hearts can't always be trusted. Jeremiah 17:9 says that our hearts are "deceitful above all things, and desperately wicked" (KJV), but "God is greater than our hearts" (1 John 3:20).

One could argue that it was more common for the great artists of the past to acknowledge the presence and gifts of God in their work—especially with images of faith being so popular in the Middle Ages and Renaissance—than it is for today's artists. Some current artists even set their work against Him. Madeleine L'Engle says that even if an artist denies God in his life, the existence of his work at its most basic point affirms Him: "Even denying God, to serve music, or painting, or words is a religious activity, whether or not the conscious mind is willing to accept that fact." She says this is because "all true art is incarnational";[13] that is, it's a process of birth-giving, of being the conduit for life, and God must be involved for new life to begin.

Still, the fact that non-believing artists are able to create works with authentic impact would have baffled Johannes Brahms, who said, "I know several young composers who are atheists. I have read their scores, and I assure you … that they are doomed to speedy oblivion, because they are utterly lacking in inspiration. Their works are purely cerebral. … No atheist has ever been or ever will be a great composer."[14]

This may or may not be true of composers, but it certainly does not seem true of the other arts. Songwriters, choreographers, playwrights, painters, and many others have accomplished much that has had impact without ever asking for help from or consciously collaborating with the Holy Spirit. This does not blow our theology; to the contrary, it points out the great love of God, who pours out not only His great gifts "on the righteous and the unrighteous" (Matt. 5:45), gifts of talent and other blessings, but also basic gifts that are so easily overlooked—nature, sunlight, the air we breathe, the functioning of our bodies. God unceasingly bestows these gifts in a constant hope that those who receive them will recognize Him and His love and at last turn their hearts in His direction. When artists or *any* of us take the gift, use it, and still deny Him—sometimes even using the gift to attack Him—His heart breaks, but His great love is reaffirmed when He once again presents the gift in hope. This is the habit of the God whose mercies are new every morning.

Seeing this part of the character of our God can motivate us, as Christian artists, not to treat our gifts lightly and not to squander them on our own selfish expressions or claim sole ownership of them. Our gifts are incredible evidence of

God's great love for us. God not only miraculously joins with us to develop our gifts, but when we offer them to Him, He also responds by giving us joy in the expression of ourselves and His love. This is the essence of collaborating with God. And this is what the non-Christian artist, though he may create great works of art, will never fully feel. He may experience a sense of partnership or guidance while he is creating, but the pure joy of knowing the Sender and Giver will never be complete. Dallas Willard said, "Jesus came to respond to the universal human need to know how to live well. He came to show us how through reliance on him we can best live in the universe as it really is."[15]

Another part of collaboration that the nonbeliever will not consistently know is collaboration with the audience. The viewer's or listener's appreciation may be fully felt, but the Holy Spirit's role of illumination probably will not be consistent. I say "probably" because God is capable of using and doing whatever He desires. But the Christian artist often gets the benefit of seeing God's Spirit move in the lives of the people to whom he presents his work. A non-Christian musician may have a good response from the live crowd he plays for; many may be very happy that he played their favorite song; but it will be rare that someone's life will actually be changed at a concert. On the other hand, the Christian musician may have the opportunity to lead someone to the Lord or to lead the crowd into worship during a concert and experience instant collaboration with God *and* his brothers and sisters as they sing.

The goal of the Christian artist is to consistently make himself and his work usable, and even if the Spirit doesn't seem to come in a big way, he is promised a blessing for his obedience (see Deut. 28).

A LOOK AT HISTORY

In our time, the arts have become monumentally influential. The musical and theatrical arts are a constant, daily part of our lives. Actors and musicians are among our biggest celebrities. Now is the time for Christian artists to pursue our destiny, to discover the powerful ways that the Spirit of the Almighty God would use us to speak to the world.

In order to better understand our place in history, it's helpful to take a quick look at the way the vocation of artist has been practiced over time. Here's an excellent overview of the last one thousand years or so in art, taken from *Women, Creativity, and the Arts*:

> In Medieval Christianity, the artist was understood to be the vehicle through which God's creative inspiration found form. Through his disciplined training and craftsmanship, the medieval Christian artist brought the implanted vision to reality, cognizant that the inspiration and the artwork were gifts from God, and that the artist was merely the vehicle for God's inspiration. Therefore, the artist took no individual credit but rather identified himself as a craftsman, not as originator or creator.
>
> With the Renaissance and its cultural shift toward the human, the artist became an individual who

originated and created new visions. The human was the measure of all things and his potential was unlimited. The ability to create works of art (literature, music, poetry, painting, sculpture) merely bolstered the renaissance artist's emerging sense of personal identity. At this same time, the public definition of genius also shifted from one favored by the gods to one of extraordinary creativity and originality. The genius brought forth masterpieces, new iconography's, and originated personal style.

In the 19th century, the romantic movement birthed a new and powerful definition of the artist as the rebel from society, the outcast who created out of a profound passion and who sacrificed everything—social status, monies, love, family— for this passion. As with the Renaissance genius, the romantic artist was the fount of originality, but unlike the Renaissance genius the romantic artist was critical of society and sought a better world. The development of "modern" or 20th century, schools of art, and their ensuing definition of the artists, were indebted to the romantic myth of the artist.[16]

I believe the modern Christian artist can embrace elements from each of these eras to develop a balanced approach to his vocation. Part of the medieval mindset, as described here, is certainly the foundation for the Christian artist. We seek God for His help and direction and dedicate our work to Him. We set a proper approach and attitude in realizing our responsibility to disciplined training and craftsmanship and in acknowledging that the inspiration and the artwork are gifts from God.

The truth we can take from the Renaissance is that God did indeed make us individuals, and we have value as unique personalities. Therefore, the way we see and interpret things has value. This perspective can be especially powerful when the artist partners with the Holy Spirit. Dallas Willard says that after a person is saved:

> The uniqueness of each individual personality remains in the beauty and goodness of its natural life. But a holy radiance rests upon it and shines through it because it is now the temple of God, the area over which the larger and higher power of God plays. An additional, spiritual life comes through the word of God as that word possesses and redirects the energies of the natural life to promote the ends of God's kingdom.[17]

It's also extremely fulfilling to let God reveal the facets of your personality to you and watch Him infuse them with meaning. Through our daily, voluntary communication with the Holy Spirit, meditation on the Bible, and interaction with our community, He sheds light and lovingly guides us away from the false, empty things that we have thought were important, focusing us on the real, core things. For example, He may show us that our obsession with a particular technique or instrument is driven by past unhealthy patterns or by pride or insecurity. When we lay these things down and shift to new directions that He seems to be leading us in, we discover the wonderful peace and rest for the righteous that replaces anxiety. In fact, this revelation that the old ways must change was the case with one of the quintessential artists of the Renaissance, Michelangelo. At the age of 72, after having lost the love of his life without even having kissed her on the cheek, he came to the realization that his humanistic approach to art had been a "great mistake."[18] He had tried to "rise [to heaven] through the contemplative exaltation of beauty." He recanted:

> My life's journey has finally arrived, after a stormy sea, in a fragile boat, at the common port, through which all must pass to render an account and explanation of their every act, evil and devout. So now I fully recognize how my fond imagination, which made art for me an idol and a tyrant, was laden with error.... Neither painting nor sculpting can any longer quieten my soul, turned now to that divine love which on the cross, to embrace us, opened wide its arms."[19]

Michelangelo devoted the next and final 20 years of his life to art—poems, drawings, sculptures, and buildings—for the glory of God.

The truth we can take from the romantic artist is that sometimes we will be at odds with current culture. We may be called to a prophetic stance, one that may require sacrifice in order to persevere and deliver the message God is giving us. Steve Turner says:

> The Christian artist will often be an irritant, disturbing the anthropocentric view of the world that fallen nature naturally gravitates toward. Just

as people think they have removed God from all consideration of a particular question, the Christian annoyingly puts him back on the agenda in some way. And when God is back on the agenda, people are forced to deal with him, even if only to try to marginalize him again.[20]

THE MIRACULOUS PRIVILEGE

So, all artists are wired to listen, but the Christian artist is in a unique position. He is better equipped to listen than the non-Christian because he can do it with an understanding of and a relationship with the One who is speaking. And because of this relationship, he is enabled to ask for help and illumination. He has the miraculous privilege of inviting God to work with him and of pitching in on projects that God is working on. This all happens through an invitation, a request for God to enter into our creative process. Certainly, He is already there in that He lives in us and He is omnipresent, but this is an invitation for specific intervention. This invitation is more than just a request for help; it is also an act of surrendering our will, of letting God's guidance and desires take precedence over our preferences and plans. It is humbling ourselves in a conscious attempt to learn to hear and to be led by His voice. It is the key that unlocks the door to divine inspiration.

Over the centuries, there have been a number of creative people who understood this concept of collaboration. We'll take a look at some of their stories in Chapter 5, but first we'll examine how God has woven creativity and art into His Word.

It's no mistake that you are an artist.

*God designed you to bring His messages to the
world through collaboration with Him.*

*And He has a unique plan for you
that will bring the creative fulfillment
you've always hoped for.*

Offer Him everything—

*talent, skill, and personality—
and tell Him you are ready to collaborate.
Then take some time and see what He says.*

CHAPTER 4

THE ART OF THE BIBLE

God is really only another artist. He invented the giraffe, the elephant, and the cat. He has no real style. He just keeps trying other things.

—Pablo Picasso[1]

THERE IS NO DOUBT—when you look at everything that's been created—that God enjoys beauty. He is the ultimate Artist, having come up with more beautiful ways to express Himself in creation than we can comprehend.

But He didn't stop at revealing Himself in creation. He also put it down in black and white (and red) in an incredible literary work of art—His Word. The Bible is, in fact, "living and active" (see Heb. 4:12) through the Holy Spirit. What a sweet thing it is to finally realize how real and immediate the Spirit can make the Word! This is a practical example of finding divine inspiration through collaboration. He will bring a work of art to life when we invite Him to it, both in the creation process and in our interaction with what has already been created.

In fifth grade, my daughter's Bible lessons at her Christian school became difficult for her, with lots of summaries and "Why do you think—?" questions. As she was struggling to make sense of it all, I suggested that, before she worked on a lesson, she could ask the Holy Spirit to help her understand; then she could read the entire Bible chapter straight through. There was a remarkable difference in her comprehension from that point on, and she no longer needed my help on every question. The Holy Spirit made the Word come alive for her.

Not only is the Bible a living, inspired, collaborative work of art, but it also contains many instances of the Holy Spirit indwelling and empowering the arts and artisans. Francis Schaeffer talked about this in his excellent little book *Art in the Bible*. He points out that while Moses was on Sinai receiving the commandments, God also gave him specific instructions about every aspect of the tabernacle, including the art in it. Art was to be present in the holiest area of the house of God and on the Ark of the Covenant. "Make two cherubim out of hammered gold at the ends of the cover" (Exod. 25:18). God goes on to describe exactly what they were to look like. Angels would seem to be an acceptable image to have in His presence, but He goes a step further to include images of nature, flowers, blossoms, and the like on the candlesticks that are in the Holy of Holies. Interestingly, these things were to be seen and enjoyed only by the chief priest and God Himself. Schaeffer points out that God reaffirmed His interest in artistic beauty later when He gave David the plans for the temple, which Solomon built. Second Chronicles 3:6 says: "And he [Solomon] garnished [covered] the house with precious stones for beauty" (KJV). Schaeffer writes, "Notice this carefully: The temple was covered with precious stones for beauty. There was no pragmatic reason for the precious stones. They had no utilitarian purpose. God simply wanted beauty in the temple. God is interested in beauty."[2]

INSPIRED PERSONAL EXPRESSION

The art of the Bible has plenty of room for the expression of man, under the influence of the Holy Spirit, as well. David may be the prime example. His psalms explore the highest praise of his God but also the deepest questioning and feelings of despair. And it was all under the banner of the Holy Spirit. David testifies in Second Samuel 23:2, "The Spirit of the Lord spake by me, and His word was upon my tongue" (KJV). One of the most stunning examples of this is found in Psalm 22, which begins with the prophetic words "My God, my God, why have you forsaken me?"—words that would later be echoed by God's Son at the darkest hour of His human existence.

David the man cried out of the depths of his own pain and confusion, lamenting that God didn't even hear him: "O my God, I cry out by day, but you do not answer, by night, and am not silent" (Ps. 22:2). But God did recognize and hear those cries, and in fact treasured them. And by having His Son speak them, He was saying to everyone who has ever cried out in pain and everyone who ever will that it is OK. He hears and cares. In fact, the intense feeling that David was experiencing and expressing with wild imagery like, "Dogs have surrounded me; a band of evil men has encircled me, they have pierced my hands and feet" (Ps. 22:16) turned out to be not only Holy Spirit inspired but also prophetically accurate! And this was all articulated in a work of art! David, the poet-musician, was expressing his humanity—under the influence of the Holy Spirit—with lyrics and music.

God inspired David personally, and He also directed him to bring music into the forefront of service to the Lord. First Chronicles 25 lists the names of the men who were chosen to minister in music at the temple, 288 in all. They were set apart for "the ministry of prophesying, accompanied by harps, lyres and cymbals" (1 Chron. 25:1). J.S. Bach wrote in the margin of his personal biblical commentary, "This chapter is the true foundation for all God-pleasing music. ...Splendid proof that ...music was instituted by the Spirit of God through David."[3]

But Spirit-inspired music was not only an expression of worship and service; it also was used as a weapon against evil. Second Chronicles 20 records that a large army came to Judah to destroy it. Desperate, King Jehosaphat proclaimed a fast. Everyone from Judah came together to seek the Lord. The king prayed, beginning, "O Lord, God of our fathers, are you not God who is in heaven?" (2 Chron. 20:6) and ending with:

But now here are men from Ammon, Moab and Mount Seir, whose territory you would not allow Israel to invade when they came from Egypt; so they turned away from them and did not destroy them. See how they are repaying us by coming to drive us out of the possession you gave us as an inheritance. O our God, will you not judge them? For we have no power to face this vast army that is attacking us. We do not know what to do, but our eyes are upon you (2 Chron. 20:10-12).

I love that prayer! So honest. So desperate, needy, and dependent. That is what we need to learn to do naturally as Christians in any situation and specifically as creative people in our projects. (This is seeking the Kingdom!)

While the people were in the position of listening after the king's prayer, the Spirit of the Lord came upon one of the Levites (who happened to be in the family of the "sons of Asaph," used by the Holy Spirit to give us many of the psalms). The powerful word that came forth was encouragement of the highest order. "Do not fear or be dismayed because of this great multitude; for the battle is not yours but God's.... Station yourselves, stand and see the salvation of the Lord on your behalf, O Judah and Jerusalem" (2 Chron. 20:15,17 NASB). At this, everyone bowed their faces to the ground except the Levites who "stood up to praise the Lord God of Israel, with a very loud voice" (2 Chron. 20:19 NASB). They got up early in the morning and the king appointed—with the people's counsel—those who were to "sing to the Lord and to praise Him for the splendor of His holiness as they went before the army saying:

'Give thanks to the Lord, for His love endures forever'" (2 Chron. 20:21).

The Holy Spirit partnered with them and Second Chronicles 20:22-23 tells us what happened:

> *As they began to sing and praise, the Lord set ambushes against the men of Ammon, Moab and Mount Seir who were invading Judah, and they were defeated. The men of Ammon and Moab rose up against the men from Mount Seir, to destroy and annihilate them. After they finished slaughtering the men from Seir, they helped to destroy one another* (2 Chronicles 20:22-23).

Incredible! The Israelites even wrapped it all up with a jam session for the Lord: "They came to Jerusalem with harps, lyres and trumpets to the house of the Lord. And the dread of God was on all the kingdoms of the lands when they heard that the Lord had fought against the enemies of Israel" (2 Chron. 20:28-29 NASB).

This is one of the many instances of the Holy Spirit collaborating with people to use the arts to accomplish His plan. Think about all the symbolism in the Bible that involved works of art, including Noah's incredible ark (architecture), the bronze serpent Moses made for the Israelites to look upon and be healed (sculpture), and David's dance. Then there are the divinely appointed crafts-men like Bezalel. Exodus 31:2-5 says of him, "I have filled him with the spirit of God, with skill, ability and knowledge in all kinds of crafts—to make artistic designs for work in gold, silver and bronze, to cut and set stones, to work in wood, and to engage in all kinds of craftsmanship."

JESUS THE ARTIST

We know that Jesus did everything He did through the power of the Holy Spirit, so seeing His use of the arts in storytelling is especially interesting. Steve Turner does an excellent job of describing this in *Imagine: A Vision for Christians in the Arts*:

> Even the most familiar words of Jesus are made memorable by what we would now refer to as literary techniques. The truths he was communicating were so vast that they couldn't be contained in plain speech. In the Sermon on the Mount he used aphorism ("Where your treasure is, there your heart will be also," Matthew 6:21), anaphora (the repetition of "Blessed are," Matthew 5:3-11), metaphor ("You are the salt of the earth," Matthew 5:13), personification ("Tomorrow will worry about itself," Matthew 6:34), analogy ("Every tree that does not bear good fruit is cut down and thrown into the fire. Thus, by their fruit you will recognize them," Matthew 7:19-20) and hyperbole ("You hypocrite, first take the plank out of your own eye," Matthew 7:5).

Turner goes on to say:

> In his storytelling—forty parables are recorded in the Gospels—he used allegory to make spiritual points and set them in the familiar landscape of

seeds, birds, rocks, weeds, fish, vineyards, corn, watchtowers and oil lamps. When questioned by those who doubted him he often answered ambiguously. When Nicodemus flattered him about his miracles he responded with "I tell you the truth, unless a man is born again, he cannot see the kingdom of God" (John 3:3) When questioned about the legitimacy of Roman taxes he said, "Give to Caesar what is Caesar's, and to God what is God's" (Matthew 22:21). When accused by Pilate he stayed silent."[4]

Jesus' use of the arts, under the influence of the Holy Spirit, is unmistakable evidence that God wants to and will collaborate with us also as we use the arts. In fact, in John 14:12, Jesus says, "I tell you the truth, anyone who has faith in me will do what I have been doing. He will do even greater things than these, because I am going to the Father."

Artful beauty is not a low priority for God.

He loves it and filled His universe with it, and
He imbues beauty and the interpretation of it
in art with messages for us.

Messages about sin, redemption, provision,
and grace.

Ask Him to let you collaborate with Him to
bring these messages to the world.

Ask for prophetic images
with meanings that will stir hearts
and break down walls.

CHAPTER 5

HISTORICAL EXAMPLES
OF DIVINE INSPIRATION

*God made me fast. And when I run I
feel His pleasure.*
—Eric Liddell, *Chariots of Fire*

THERE WERE MANY ARTISTS AND CREATIVE PEOPLE in the past who made themselves useable and collaborated with God in their work. The people we'll look at put themselves in a position to be guided. Most of these have come to our attention because of the success of their work, but it is important to remember that worldly success is not the ultimate measure of the man or woman. To paraphrase Mother Teresa, the person who operates in loving obedience to God is the truly successful person.

In fact, there will be multitudes of surprise heroes in Heaven, unknown on earth but celebrated above. This world believes the greatest artists impact the world with work that lasts, and that is true in this realm, but this realm will eventually pass away, and then only what's done for Christ will stand. In God's Kingdom, the greatest artists may be those who were fully surrendered and obedient to Him, joyfully operating in true collaboration.

Many of the following people had the great pleasure and privilege of not only impacting the world in their time, but also storing up rewards in Heaven through willful collaboration with their God. We can learn something from each one of them

Composers in Collaboration

(Much of the material for the composers is taken from the book, *Spiritual Lives of the Great Composers*, by Patrick Cavanagh.)

The story of George Frederick Handel's (1685–1759) writing of the "Hallelujah Chorus" is one of my favorite examples of inspiration from and collaboration with the Holy Spirit.

In *Spiritual Lives of the Great Composers*, Patrick Cavanagh describes a situation where the composer was sequestered in his room for more than a week, receiving visits only from a servant who brought him food he left uneaten. Then one day, when the servant entered the composer's room, he was confronted with a weeping and emotional Handel, who had just completed the movement that would be known as the "Hallelujah Chorus." Handel cried out, "I did think I did see all heaven before me, and the great God Himself."

Cavanagh writes that much of Handel's three weeks of isolation while writing The Messiah were like this: "A friend who visited him as he composed found him sobbing with intense emotion. Later, as Handel groped for words to describe what he had experienced, he quoted Paul, saying, 'Whether I was in the body or out of the body when I wrote I know not.'"[1]

Handel turned his heart toward God and shut out all the other voices that might overpower that still, small voice. He was focused on communing with God as he did his work. The position he took in God's presence, coupled with his God-given and faithfully developed talent and the Holy Spirit's inspiration, produced one of the greatest musical expressions ever created.

Of the fruit of this work, Patrick Cavanaugh says:

Handel personally conducted more than thirty performances of Messiah. Many of these concerts were benefits for the Foundling Hospital, of which Handel was a major benefactor. The thousands of pounds that Handel's performances of the *Messiah* raised for charity led one biographer to note: "Messiah has fed the hungry, clothed the naked, and fostered the orphan...more than any other single musical production in any country." Another wrote, "Perhaps the works of no other composer have so largely contributed to the relief of human suffering."[2]

This work has had an uncanny spiritual impact on the lives of its listeners. One writer has stated that *Messiah's* music and message "has probably done more to convince thousands of mankind that there is a God about us than all the theological works ever written."[3]

Handel's example leads us to minimize the competing voices and to focus on God in our creative process.

As Patrick Cavanagh also notes in his book, a number of other composers (including Hayden, Dvorak, Mendelsonn, and Messiaen) put visible markings on their work to show that each piece was done in collaboration with and for the glory of God. The most famous may be Johann Sebastian Bach (1685–1750), who frequently put the initials J.J. (*Jesu Juva*—"Help me, Jesus") or I.N.J. (*In Nomine Jesu*—"In Jesus' Name") at the top of his compositions. At the end he would add S.D.G. (*Soli Deo Gloria*—"To God Alone, the glory"). Leann Payne says in *Listening Prayer*, "This is how a man of great genius committed his day's work to God. The fact that he wrote, as some say, the equivalent of a masterpiece per day is undoubtedly due in great part to this committal."[4] Richard Wagner later called Bach's legacy of incredible works "the most stupendous miracle in all of music."[5]

We can learn from Bach to wrap each piece of our work in prayer, prayer that might include an acknowledgment of our desperate need for help from the Savior and a humble dedication to Him of all we might create.

Cavanagh writes that Johannes Brahms (1833–97) spoke about his creative process in this way:

I will now tell you and our young friend here about my method of communicating with the Infinite, for all truly inspired ideas come from God. Beethoven, who was my ideal, was well aware of this.

When I feel the urge, I begin by appealing directly to my Maker and I first ask Him the three most important questions pertaining to our life here in this world—whence, wherefore, whither?

Straightaway the ideas flow in upon me, directly from God, and not only do I see distinct themes in my mind's eye, but they are clothed in the right forms, harmonies and orchestration.

…Jesus was the world's supreme spiritual genius, and He was conscious of appropriating the only true source of power as no one else ever was.

…Jesus Himself was very explicit about this, in saying, "Ask and it shall be given you, seek and ye shall find; knock and it shall be opened unto you." There would not be so much good music paper wasted in fruitless attempts to compose if those great precepts were better understood.[6]

This is true and can easily be translated into all other pursuits of the arts. A lot of canvas, printer's ink, studio time, etc., as well as precious energy, could be saved from fruitless attempts to create if we would ask, seek, and knock for the divinely inspired ideas.

We can learn from Brahms to ask for the Spirit to plant creative ideas in our hearts, minds, and spirits and then to wait until they come.

Many of the great composers were known for their humility, and Antonin Dvorak (1841–1904), Czechoslovakia's greatest composer, was no exception. He often focused the attention he got back on God, saying, "I simply do what God tells me to do."[7] When Franz Joseph Haydn (1732–1809) rose to thunderous applause after a performance of his masterwork, *The Creation* (the last performance he would attend before his death), he lifted his hands toward Heaven and said, "Not from me—from there, above, comes everything."[8]

WRITERS IN COLLABORATION

There have been many examples of writers being inspired by God, and as I mentioned in Chapter 1, one of the great ones is Harriet Beecher Stowe, author of *Uncle Tom's Cabin*. In our day, that book is known for its stereotypes of African Americans, but in the 1850s and 1860s, it was the most powerful argument against the evils of slavery ever published.

Stowe was a devout Christian who felt strongly that slavery should be abolished and published her views in magazines of the time. When she was asked to write a new antislavery article, a fiction piece, she struggled to come up with an idea. After a long period of writer's block, she was sitting in church one Sunday morning when she had the vision that led to *Uncle Tom's Cabin*. In *The Artist's Way*, Julia Cameron describes how this vision affected Stowe:

> For the rest of her life, Stowe was convinced that the Almighty had reached out to her, that the inspiration had been His, not her own.
>
> …She hurried home from church and, dinner forgotten, put the vision on paper, describing the scenes precisely as she had seen them. Overcome by emotion, she summoned her hungry children and read aloud what she had written. All of them wept, and one sobbed, "Oh, Mama! Slavery is the most cruel thing in the world." Any doubts about the work she still may have entertained were swept aside at that moment.[9]

Stowe experienced other moments of inspiration as the work went on for a year, each week producing a new segment to be published in *National Era* magazine. She was able to take the stories of slaves she had met—in retrospect, by divine appointment—draw from their experiences, and work them into the book. This weaving together of passion, past experiences, and inspiration from God is one of the hallmarks of the Holy Spirit's working in our creative process.

Released as a book in 1852, the stories created a greater sensation than perhaps any other book before or since. Only God could have done such incredible things through a woman who had never written a book. Later, she stated, "I could not control the story; it wrote itself. I the author of *Uncle Tom's Cabin*? No, indeed. The Lord Himself wrote it, and I was but the humblest of instruments in His hand. To Him alone should be given all the praise."[10]

SCIENTISTS AND INVENTORS IN COLLABORATION

A number of scientists and inventors of the past also led godly lives and collaborated with God in their inventions. Samuel F.B. Morse, the inventor of the telegraph—the foundation of all modern communications—acknowledged God with his immortal first words to be transmitted in Morse Code, "What hath God wrought!" What a testimony for the ages!

Morse was originally a painter who turned his creativity toward electrical impulses after an intriguing conversation on a long trip. A man named George Hervey was later said to have asked him in an interview,

> "Professor Morse, when you were making your experiments at the University, did you ever come to a standstill, not knowing what to do next?"
>
> He replied, "I've never discussed this with anyone, so the public knows nothing about it. But now that you ask me, I'll tell you frankly—I prayed for more light."
>
> "And did God give you the wisdom and the knowledge you needed?" Hervey asked.
>
> "Yes he did," said Morse. "That's why I never felt I deserved the honors that have come to me from America and Europe because of the invention associated with my name. I made a valuable application

of the use of electrical power, but it was all through God's help. It wasn't because I was superior to other scientists. When the Lord wanted to bestow this gift on mankind, He had to use someone. I'm just grateful He chose to reveal it to me."[11]

Morse also wrote in a letter to his brother Sidney:

It is His work, and He alone could have carried me thus far through all my trials and enabled me to triumph over the obstacles physical and moral which opposed me. ... I do indeed feel gratified, and it is right I should rejoice but I rejoice with fear, and I desire that a sense of dependence upon and increased obligation to the Giver of every good and perfect gift, may keep me humble, and circumspect.[12]

Scientist George Washington Carver's unique story of guidance, and the results of that guidance, had an impact on countless people throughout the south and across the country. Born in Diamond Grove, Missouri, around 1864 (no records were kept because he was a slave), Carver had a horrendous childhood, surviving the death of his sister by slave rustlers, the death of his father in a farming accident, and the disappearance of his mother after she was kidnapped and held for ransom. His owner, a godly German farmer named Moses Carver, paid the ransom with a racehorse and later adopted George and his brother and gave them his last name.

His adopted parents raised Carver and his brother to be Christians. That early teaching went deep into Carver's soul, and as an adult he developed a habit of getting up each morning at 4:00 a.m. and taking a walk with God. "During these times he prayed for guidance and help for the day's work."[13] Over time he was responsible for the development of important advances in soil regeneration through rotating crops from year to year, the development of over one hundred uses for the sweet potato (including making vinegar, glue, starch, and shoe polish), as well as finding more than three hundred important uses for the peanut. Carver's desire was to help the poor farmers of the South become more productive, and he accomplished it by asking for the guidance and inspiration of the Holy Spirit. "Without God to draw aside the curtain," he said, "I would be helpless."[14] He always kept a Bible on his desk at the Tuskegee Institute and is said to have called his laboratory "God's little workshop."

When he was asked by the Senate how he had been able to discover so many uses for the peanut, Carver explained that God's Word in Genesis 1:29 (his favorite verse) had guided him: "Then God said, 'I give you every seed-bearing plant on the face of the whole earth and every tree that has fruits with seeds in it. They will be yours for food.'" Carver believed that God had made "the beautiful world of plants and animals for man's delight and use, and that it was man's duty to discover as many of those uses as possible for the benefit of mankind."[15] His presentation led Congress to restrict the import of peanuts from other countries and saved the American peanut industry.

George Washington Carver's example encourages us to consistently and humbly seek God's guidance. This man's devotion to God and the unmistakable evidence of His guidance in Carver's work was acknowledged in the citation for the Roosevelt Medal he received in 1939, which reads, "To a scientist humbly seeking the guidance of God and a liberator to men of the white race as well as the black."

ARTISTS IN COLLABORATION

Artists have frequently been used to display God's glory in their collaboration with Him. One such example is Fra Angelico (1387–1455), an excellent Renaissance painter and priest who "some people claim, never set his hand to a brush without saying a prayer."[16] God answered his prayers. In *The History of Art*, Volker Gebhardt calls Angelico a "thoroughly intellectual painter, whose works in fact represent extremely sophisticated experiments in the development of painting."[17] Much of his work was done in and around Florence, but the pope sent for him as his fame grew and had him paint the chapel of the Vatican palace. The pope, seeing that Angelico was a holy, quiet, and modest man, offered him the archbishopric of Florence when that position became vacant. But Angelico believed another priest was more qualified and recommended him instead; an incredible act of humility. "He applied himself continuously to his painting and never wanted to work on anything but Holy subjects. He could have been rich but cared little about wealth; on the contrary, he used to say that true wealth was nothing but being content with little."[18]

"It was his habit never to retouch or redo any of his paintings," Vasari writes, "but, rather, always to leave them just as they had turned out the first time, since he believed (according to what he said) that this was God's will."[19]

— 71 —

Fra Angelico was humble and lived with simple trust, yet worked to create the best artwork possible. That's a great standard to live up to.

HISTORICAL COLLABORATION IN SUMMARY

There are countless flashes of God's collaboration with and through others in history—painters like Michelangelo, Da Vinci, and Rembrandt, whose paintings sometimes seemed touched by God; scientists like Issac Newton, who said that all his discoveries were a result of answered prayer, and Blaise Pascal, who did his work to the glory of God. There was Bible translator J.B. Phillips, who said he felt like electricity was going through him when he wrote his translation of the Bible, and many more.

It should be noted that although the men and women mentioned in this chapter were all highly acclaimed and talented, there is just as much honor to God in the art or creativity of the person who is not as talented or whose talents are not so well developed. God enjoys the authentic expression that any of His children offer to Him. That it may have an effect on the world is solely the work of the Holy Spirit. Bob Briner says, "We do not have to be the best to be effective, but we do have to be at our best."[20]

You may be the next person to leave a legacy that touches the world. All it could take is living out the decision to collaborate with God in what He wants to do. You get there by learning to listen.

*You have a place in history
that no one else can fill.
God planned good works
(and work) for you to do
even before you were born.
Your destiny is to collaborate with God
in the work He leads you to,
and your willful collaboration ushers
His Kingdom into the world.
Don't worry about dreaming big dreams,
He has that handled.
Commit to living purely
and to quietly listening for His voice every day,
and see where He takes you.*

CHAPTER 6

DEVELOPING A LISTENING LIFESTYLE

I would rather a thousand times be five
minutes at the feet of Christ than listen a
lifetime to all the wise men in the world.
—D.L. Moody[1]

WE'VE ESTABLISHED THAT GOD DESIGNED humans to collaborate, that artists are people designed to listen and express what they observe in collaboration with the Holy Spirit, and that there are rich biblical and historical examples of this. Now it's time to look at some practical ways that we can move into a *listening lifestyle*. At times we Christians are challenged to live up to a certain standard and then left to try to achieve that without the benefit of practical application or discipleship. In this chapter, you'll be exposed to some wonderful spiritual tools that can help you build a better listening relationship with God in your life and work.

"But seek first His kingdom and His righteousness, and all these things will be added to you" (Matt. 6:33 NASB). My former pastor, Sean Tienhaara, was fond of saying that having the attitude of Matthew 6:33 boils down to praying the short prayer, "God, what do you want me to do?" in all situations, or "How would you like me to use my time, resources, and will in this moment?" Most Christians have probably prayed this at one time or another, but we often have difficulty hearing God's answer. Maybe He just expects us to do what seems right.

Or maybe He is speaking to us, but we just aren't listening.

Walter Wangerin Jr., in *Whole Prayer*, says that our communication with God is not complete until we have listened to Him. Wangerin says, "We speak, He listens. He speaks, we listen."[2] But what does it look like to listen to God? Should we expect to hear a voice or angels softly singing? How can we know God is speaking to us and not our subconscious or (yikes!) satan.

For me, listening to God can take many forms. Sometimes He'll speak to me through His Word and sometimes through people or circumstances. But when I'm alone, it is mostly through expectant waiting, a concept that requires letting go of my busyness and restlessness. It means being silent in a prayerful attitude and expecting His Spirit to be present, to speak in a still, small voice. I'll usually write down in my journal what I think He is saying.

I don't think I've ever heard angels singing, or a booming, audible voice, and my own thoughts and outside influences can make it difficult to discern what God saying. There have been times when satan has tried to throw a lie into the mix. We'll talk about all these situations later. But the benefits of pushing through and listening to what God is communicating to me have been monumental, miraculous, and life changing!

There is a progression to becoming adept at hearing God's voice. Just like any human relationship, the more we dialogue with God, giving Him time to speak to us, the better we'll know Him and recognize His voice. The Bible is full of practical steps that will lead us toward holiness and more freedom in Him. And those in turn will bring more confidence to relax and listen for His voice. Let's take a look at some of those steps and how we can apply them.

Romans 12:1-2 clearly lays out the path to knowing God's will and hearing what He has to say.

Therefore, I urge you, brothers, in view of God's mercy, to offer your bodies as living sacrifices, holy and pleasing to God—this is your spiritual act of worship. Do not conform any longer to the pattern of this world, but be transformed by the renewing of your mind. Then you will be able to test and approve what God's will is—His good, pleasing and perfect will.

As you'll see, I'm a big fan of breaking Scripture down into steps in order to mine the deep things that are present. We'll do that with these verses. Here are the steps:

1. "Therefore, I urge you, brothers, in view of God's mercy...." Develop a true and personal understanding of the mercy of God.

2. "...To offer your bodies as living sacrifices, holy and pleasing to God—this is your spiritual act of worship." As an act of worship (something you can give voluntarily), offer your body—your natural life—as a sacrifice.

3. "Do not conform any longer to the pattern of this world...." Make a break from the attitudes and ways of the world.

4. "...But be transformed by the renewing of your mind." Put yourself in a position for God to change you.

5. "Then you will be able to test and approve what God's will is—His good, pleasing and perfect will." Do these things and you'll be able to hear and know God's will in your specific circumstances.

Let's expand on these.

1. "Therefore, I urge you, brothers, in view of God's mercy...." Develop a true and personal understanding of the mercy of God.

The best way to get a true understanding of God's mercy is through immersing ourselves in the "things of God" (the Word, prayer, and community), putting ourselves in a place where we can receive daily insight and even revelation from the Holy Spirit. As He meets us and brings our faith to life, we'll begin to see more and more of His mercy. Madeleine L'Engle says, "If our lives are truly 'hid with Christ in God,' the astounding thing is that this hiddenness is revealed in all that we do and say and write."[3] We can also get a personal understanding of God's mercy through totally screwing up! Then, when we turn to Him in desperation, He extends His mercy in a way we don't deserve and couldn't have worked hard enough to get. And that's when we really begin to understand how much God loves us like a tender Father.

There is something so wonderful about the dawn of a new day. It's the starting point of the daily understanding of God's mercy. It's His merciful design that sleep brings new perspective, the sunshine new hope, and our hearts can say, "This is the day you have made." As it says in Lamentations, "It is of the Lord's mercies that we are not consumed, because his compassions fail not. They are new every morning..." (Lam. 3:22-23 KJV). It is an example of God's mercy that you don't even have to believe in Him to benefit from the mercy of the new day's renewing effect!

We demonstrate that we have a good understanding of God's mercy when we make a point to meet Him daily and worship Him for it. Make no mistake; getting a listening lifestyle has its foundation in daily time with God—learning and being honest in the presence of the Father. Some people say it doesn't matter if you spend time with God in the morning or at night—just do it. There is truth to that, but I believe morning devotional time has the most benefit. We run the risk of getting off track if our day has not been consecrated to Him and His guidance sought before the day has begun. Jesus often modeled this when He withdrew in the morning and spent time with His Father. I once heard a well-known pastor say that our mission should be to get filled up with God's mercy at the beginning of the day and just pour it out all day long until we are empty.

2. "…To offer your bodies as living sacrifices, holy and pleasing to God—this is your spiritual act of worship." As an act of worship (something you can give voluntarily), offer your body—your natural life—as a sacrifice.

Oswald Chambers puts this better than anyone when he says that this is a call to give up our "right to ourselves." "It is not a question of giving up sin, but of giving up my right to myself, my natural independence, my self will."[4] "My individuality remains, but my primary motivation for living and the nature that rules me are radically changed."[5] "If you will give God your right to yourself, He will make a holy experiment out of you—and His experiments always succeed."[6]

This sacrifice, this self-denial, is not for the sake of becoming more pious and righteous, but it is for worship, unique worship that only you can give. And though self-denial is often painful, it is most certainly pain with reward, guaranteed rewards in the next life, but often rewards here and now—in peace, in knowing God in a deeper way, in sensing that we have done what we can, in a new appreciation for the blessings that come from obedience.

Beyond following the guidelines in the Bible, sacrifice calls for listening to what the Holy Spirit is calling you to on a daily basis. It's interesting to note that offering ourselves as a living sacrifice does not mean we need to deny everything that feels good to us. In fact, often God may be calling you to do something other than make the seemingly obvious sacrifice in a situation. Say your church is offering an overseas missions trip and you think you should go. Several spiritual leaders you look up to are going, and it seems like the right thing to do. It will require you to sacrifice your time, money, and vacation days at work. After some overdue prayer-retreat time, you realize God is telling you to stay home instead and work on something He's been speaking to you about. Though it looks like the good thing to do would be go and make the sacrifice, the better thing is to obey. The Bible teaches that to obey is better than sacrifice (see 1 Sam. 15:22). In fact, sometimes obedience that doesn't make much sense may be the sacrifice God is calling us to—the sacrifice of our logic or plans and the giving up of our right to understand.

Of course, the best way to know how and what God may be calling us to sacrifice is to listen to the Holy Spirit. At one time He may be guiding you to fast; another time He may bless you with a wonderful dinner. One Friday night He may be calling you to stay home and read and pray; another Friday He might give you the release to stay out late with friends and go dancing! And wonderfully, being able to hear this kind of direction will be one of the real by-products of sacrifice.

3. "Do not conform any longer to the pattern of this world...." Make a break from the attitudes and ways of the world.

Live in the world but not of it. Yes, we must avoid the sins of the world: lust, murder, lying, etc. But the real "pattern of the world" is in its attitudes. I'm not talking about being happy all the time, but the way we deal with what comes our way. I remember, after I really became immersed in the Word and let God change whatever He wanted to in me, realizing how the attitudes and approach of the world are at odds with God's approach to so many things. I'll talk about that a little later.

An artist who was visiting my church came up with this list of attitudes that come from the world:

> If you are living in fear…then you're living like the world.
> If you are driving by pride…then you are living like the world.
> If you see injustice and turn a blind eye…you are living like the world.
> If you love those who love you, but curse your enemies…then you are living like the world.
> If you have bought into the dog-eat-dog mentality…you are living like the world.[7]

This is not an exhaustive list—you probably could add several thoughts of your own— but it is an eye-opening way to identify the subtle worldly attitudes that can creep in.

If we ask Him, God will move us to see His perspective and empower us to live in it. But it's not a change that we can make on our own. The shift to conforming to God's pattern comes only through pursuing step 4.

4. "...But be transformed by the renewing of your mind." Put yourself in a position for God to change you.

Your mind is only transformed by the power of the Holy Spirit, because He is the only one who can truly renew it. The Holy Spirit does this transforming work when we collaborate with Him while reading the Word of God. Dallas Willard says:

> Just think for a moment about what happens when you wash a dirty shirt: the water and laundry soap move through the fibers of the shirt material and carry out the dirt lodged within those fibers. When we come to God our minds and hearts are like that dirty shirt, cluttered with false beliefs and attitudes, deadly feelings, past deeds and misguided plans, hopes and fears. The word of God— primarily the gospel of his kingdom and of the life and the death of Jesus on our behalf—enters our mind and brings new life through faith. As we open our entire life to this new power and as those sent by God minister the word to us, the word moves into every part of our personality, just like the water and soap move through the shirt's fibers. God's word pushes out and replaces all that is false and opposed to Gods' purposes in creating us and putting us in our unique place on earth.

> We are transformed by the renewing of our minds and thus are able to 'discern what is the will of God—what is good and acceptable and perfect'. Hearing God becomes a reliably clear and practical

matter for the mind that is transformed by this washing of the word.[8]

He will also transform and renew our minds in our prayer time, while we seek Him. These two things, the Bible and listening prayer, are the greatest ways that God can transform and renew our minds. The Word, by the Holy Spirit, is sharper in us than any sword and cuts into and reveals the deepest parts of us. And in prayer, the Spirit will often whisper things to us that leapfrog over issues and problems that might normally hold us back from being healed and transformed. Sometimes the Holy Spirit will speak a word during prayer—alone or with others—that saves years of mental turmoil and therapy!

5. "Then you will be able to test and approve what God's will is—His good, pleasing and perfect will." Do these things and you'll be able to hear and know God's will in your specific circumstances.

We're talking about more than knowing God's will that's stated in the Bible—though it is essential to have that as a foundation. I believe this applies to knowing God's will for you in specific situations! Do these things and you'll be more free to hear His voice.

I should make it clear that a listening lifestyle is not about getting every little direction, all the time, from God. As we put ourselves more in alignment with His Word and walk in His attitudes, we'll become more in tune with His will and be able to hear His guidance more easily. For me, there are some times when He does direct me in the smallest details; other times I don't receive detailed instruction but go forward in faith, inviting Him into the process, committing my steps to Him, and remaining sensitive to His voice as I walk.

By following this process from Romans 12:1-2, knowing His will and hearing His voice in our lives can become a vibrant reality instead of a theory or far-off aspiration.

A Path to Hearing God

If you want to hear from God, get truly honest with Him. Then trust Him to do whatever He wants.

For years I foundered in my morning devotions. The excuses were easy to come by: I couldn't get up to do them because I'm not a morning person; my mind would always wander; I didn't seem to get much out of them; I didn't really know how to study the Bible. I still struggle with these things, but now my devotions are almost always fruitful. This change came because of a number of reasons, the first being that I quit messing around with my relationship with the Father. More than 20 years of fluctuating levels of commitment to and concentration on my faith had accumulated into a load of spiritual misconceptions and had created callousness. I thought I knew how to live a Christian life, but when the shattering crisis of separation and divorce blindsided me, I got desperate.

And that's when my faith became real. The crisis effectively nuked all of my old presumptions about life and faith, so much so that I often felt like I had two choices: death or His touch. In my desperate honesty, He did meet me, and I found out that He had been waiting for a long time. All the questions about faith had gone unanswered because of my misconception that being a "good Christian" meant just accepting things that were laid on the table. I also put myself in a position to let God search through my false assumptions, spiritual pride, spiritual laziness, and carnal thinking.

I started praying only honest prayers. I didn't pray "safe" stuff, but instead expressed real thoughts and feelings and asked for dangerous things—things that I really needed. I tried to really depend on His provision instead of taking care of everything myself and leaving only the "impossible" things to Him. I thought, *If God is real and He cares about my life, then let's do it!* I decided to open myself up and ask Him to work, without setting up all my contingency plans in case He didn't come through. By the way, contingency plans are one of the reasons why "it's easier for a camel to go through the eye of a needle than for a rich man to enter the Kingdom of God" (Matt. 19:24). Money can buy you more options. You may think you don't need to depend on God because you have other ways to accomplish things. Jesus' heart was close to the poor because they *knew* they needed His help! We need to learn this attitude in order to develop a listening lifestyle.

Another thing I did was to look for my Father to use the Bible to speak to me. I got wild and started to flip at random on occasion, praying for the Holy Spirit to guide. I started to ask the Holy Spirit to bring understanding before I read or during reading. I asked Him to bring illumination, even revelation, when I hit a difficult or troubling passage. And He did! "But the Counselor, the Holy Spirit, whom the

Father will send in my name, will teach you all things and remind you of everything I have said to you"(John 14:26). Someone once said the Bible is the only book that comes with its own teacher.

THE JOY OF JOURNALING

As my spiritual life was being reformed, I started to journal in a new and honest way. I write down bits and pieces of what I think God might be saying to me: verses of Scripture, lines from devotionals, encouragement or thoughts from other people, even prophetic or inspired words—along with the deeper cries of my heart: angry questions for God, the anguish of struggles, the wonder of answered prayers. Everything goes in my journal; it doesn't need to make sense or be a "thus sayeth the Lord." Time and perspective make it fairly easy to discern what is real and what is nonsense. "If I can write things out I can see them, and they are no longer trapped within my own subjectivity."[9]

This is not a journal for anyone else's eyes, and I put the words *Private Journal* on the outside. It seems juvenile, but it's effective. I don't leave my journal lying around to tempt the curious. I pray for the Father to protect it from prying eyes.

Even though it is sometimes inconvenient to take such precautions, it is nothing compared to the hundreds of joys that God has given in the reading of the entries. This is a treasure, and it has helped my life make sense in the most desperate of times. To look back on an entry and see the work of the Lord in my thoughts or life—even though I may not have recognized it at the time—is an incredible blessing. I see the threads of His leading and His voice winding through the months and the years. Madeleine L'Engle said: "I am still in the process of growing up, but I will make no progress if I lose any of myself along the way."[10]

Prayers of desperation that have been answered build my faith; changed situations with people I've prayed for over the years amaze me. Deep revelations that God deposited in times of seeking often inspire me more in retrospect than they did at the time of writing. This journal is the history of a glorious relationship, a never-ending love, and a constant faithfulness, *and* it is also a uniquely fulfilling form of creative collaboration! I express myself to God; He expresses Himself to me; we create a living, growing relationship. What a blessing to experience creativity in such a context!

Julia Cameron, in *The Artist's Way*, talks about the importance of journaling for the creative person. She has her students write three "morning pages" every day as a way of getting past the internal "censor" that constantly nags artists, telling us "we can't" or "we aren't," or whatever. She suggests that the pages can be about anything or nothing, but they are a way to clear the mind so we can get on with the business of creativity. "The morning pages will teach you to stop judging and just let yourself write."[11]

It's good to remember that your prayer journal can look like anything you want it to. Not having to judge it and instead just letting yourself write and express is *so* freeing spiritually, mentally, emotionally, and creatively. This makes it completely different from one of those journals from some pious historical figure that you hear quoted, or the kind that you had to keep for English class in high school. This is between you and God, so you can be completely honest.

Even though there is not a "correct" way to keep a personal prayer journal, there is a structural cornerstone you can build it on that will keep it from being more than just ramblings. It's tremendously helpful to build it on the Lord's Prayer. This awesome gift from Jesus' lips is often overlooked or oversimplified.

In reading Leanne Payne's *Listening Prayer*, the importance of practicing the Lord's Prayer became clear to me. It is an outline to guide us into confidence in seeking the Father, to know that we are coming before Him in a manner that is pleasing to Him. It's difficult to improve on what Payne has written, so I'll borrow from her heavily. She suggests that you divide the front of your journal into sections (which is one of the reasons I always use a loose-leaf binder for my journals), each focusing on a part of the Lord's Prayer. You then put your specific requests and thoughts into each section. So your devotional time takes on a sort of pattern that could look something like this:

- Pray through the Lord's Prayer sections with the specific thoughts and requests you've written down. Add any others that come to you.

- Then, ask God to open the Word to you as you read a passage and meditate on it.

- Write anything down in your journal section (which might be after the Lord's Prayer sections) that comes to you about what you've read and prayed.

- Then, ask God to speak to you about whatever is on your heart and/or whatever He wants.

- Get quiet and listen. Write down what you feel He is speaking to you.

- Test it against the Bible, or get a trusted person's opinion on it if you need to.

This is a pattern that revolutionized my spiritual life!

Now, let's return to the elements of the Lord's Prayer and their relevance to a growing spiritual life. Essentially, if you dissect the prayer into specific parts and try to get at the spirit of each part, this is what you might find:

1. "Our Father, which art in heaven, hallowed be Thy name" (Matt. 6:9 KJV). This is "praise and thanksgiving" to the Father; acknowledging Him for what He has done and created. It is putting ourselves aside for a moment, taking a deep breath, and getting our perspective back. Psalm 46:10 says, "Be still and know that I am God...." It's also thanking Him for the things He has done specifically in our lives, recounting those blessings. If you were following the pattern above, you'd create a section in the front of your journal that would be titled with this part of the verse and labeled "Praise and Thanksgiving." You might write down everything you are thankful for and make that the beginning of your prayer every day.

2. "Thy kingdom come, Thy will be done in earth as it is in heaven" (Matt. 6:10 KJV). In the pattern I'm talking about, you would label this section "Intercession," and it would go in the front of your journal also. Intercession is praying for other people and their needs, asking God to work out His will in specific and general circumstances. Notice this comes before we ever mention our needs. This part of the prayer can also be a real faith-builder if you keep a list of the people you are praying for and write the answers to the prayers next to their names. Putting a date that you started praying for them and the date the answer came is also incredibly interesting. This section also will help you see more clearly how God uses us in others' lives and how He has made us to interact with Him.

3. "Give us this day our daily bread" (Matt. 6:11 KJV). This section would follow the other two at the front of your journal. This section is all about you; it's where you take all of your personal requests and just lay them before God.

Here are some gems of thought on this from Leanne Payne:

> There are those, however, who think personal petition to be somehow inferior or even selfish. But the truth is that we need to pay attention to the heart's personal needs and desires, and take care to spread them out before the Lord: Prayer in the Christian sense does not...accept the idea of a higher stage of prayer where petition is left behind. The progress that is seen in the spiritual life is from the prayer of rote to the prayer of the heart.[12]

As we wait for the Lord we fill this section with our personal petitions, great and small, that require ongoing prayer and even perseverance.[13]

It is important, therefore, to ask always for God's mind and even his most perfect will on our petitions. To persevere with God in this way is a needful thing.[14]

4. "And forgive us our debts, as we forgive our debtors" (Matt. 6:12 KJV). This is the part where we daily repent and forgive, a real essential to clear communication with God. It follows the previous sections in the front of your journal and may be the most important part of your daily prayer. You may think you are squared away in this area, but ask God to show you anyone you have something against, anyone whose actions toward you have been a continual source of hurt. Often, what the Father is asking us to do is just to turn our will toward forgiveness, even if the miracle and grace of forgiving a certain person is beyond us. When we let Him, He will work this out over time and through this prayer. It is His work. We'll talk more about forgiveness later.

5. "And lead us not into temptation..." (Matt. 6:13 KJV). What are your temptations? Really? What things do you push back in the dark places of your mind? Lust? Self-centeredness? Pride? Arrogance? Racial thoughts? Ask God to help you drag these things into the light and identify them. Then write them down in this section and pray about them daily. You may be amazed at how this "Temptations" section will help you become a more authentic person by fostering a real honesty toward God and toward other people. Our Father already knows everything about us, and as

we get honest, the realization comes that He is the only one who can lead us to real change.

6. "...But deliver us from evil: For Thine is the kingdom, and the power and the glory, for ever and ever. Amen" (Matt. 6:13 KJV). Recognize that we are in a battle but that God provides us with protection (see Eph. 6:13-18). Leanne Payne says, "This does not mean that we won't suffer, but rather that good will come from the suffering; it will be redemptive in contrast to being merely remedial."[15] This part of the prayer is really about crushing the lies that satan would try to bind us up with, telling us we can do nothing in the face of evil. James wrote, "Submit yourselves, then, to God. Resist the devil, and he will flee from you. Come near to God and He will come near to you" (James 4:7-8).

Of course, the Lord's Prayer is not a "required" form for communicating with God. It is foundational, and recommended by Jesus, but there are many times when we need to just cry out, or to dialogue with the Father like we would with our friends—or to just be silent.

In the pattern I mentioned earlier, after I've prayed through the sections of the Lord's Prayer, I might read a passage from the Bible and meditate on it, if I haven't done that yet. Then I journal thoughts on that passage or whatever is on my heart. Finally, I stop to listen.

I was a Christian for 25 years before I really began giving God time to speak to me on a daily basis. I had devotional time in varying degrees over those years, but there were only a couple of times I could say that I knew God had spoken to me. Both were on walks while I was praying and thinking, in a position of listening. One time was after I saw *Forrest Gump* to review it. The film so touched me that I felt compelled to take a walk and ended up praying about my life. I felt God speak very clearly to my mind and say that I needed to help my wife find out who she was. It was a profound moment. Unfortunately, I let it slip away, and two years later the marriage ended. That taught me a lesson that I've had to relearn many times: when God speaks, do something about what He says.

As a side note, though the disintegration of my marriage was not something I wanted and though it was profoundly painful, God brought about the book you are reading through seeking Him in that pain. And after years of waiting, He also brought me a wonderful new spouse, Danielle. I believe that marriage should be honored and that everything possible should be done to sustain it, and in my case, I believe that's what I did with my first marriage. But in the end, it was out of my hands. For many years, I was confused about why this happened, but now I see God's glorious grace in the situation and how He worked this out for my good and the good of our family, just as He promises to do for all of His children.

As I said in earlier chapters, everything changed after crises in my life mercifully drove me to cling to the Father. But the biggest change in my prayer life came when I just got quiet and listened. After all the years of telling God what I needed, asking Him to bless me, and then hurrying on my way, I finally stepped into a dialogue with Him. It was a revelation to expect to hear from God. I decided I would not think it was strange if He spoke; in fact, I'd consider it normal.

One thing I always do when preparing to listen to God, besides cleaning the slate of sin and unforgiveness, is to ask Him to protect my listening time. I ask that His angels would surround me and that I'd hear vertically from Him, not horizontally from myself or from the enemy. Then I get quiet.

Learning to listen is really a process. It takes personal experimentation, learning from material you read or hear, and comparing notes with other mature Christians. You'll find that some days you seem to be walking in the Spirit like a saint; other days it seems that God is not speaking at all. Some days you may hear profound prophetic words, some days just nonsense from your own issues, and some days nothing at all. That's the nature of being a flawed human vessel; we don't hear or get everything right. But a wonderful thing about faith is that everything doesn't always have to make sense.

I'll try to paraphrase a story I read of a man who decided to listen to God in his quiet time to see what He had to say. All he heard was "I love you." He thought, *I could have made that up myself.* For weeks all he heard was "I love you." He got very frustrated, telling God, "I know You love me! Don't You have anything else to say?" He sensed God say, "Do you? Do you really know I love you?" The man broke down in tears, and healing began to flow through issues and misconceptions he'd had about how God felt about him. The Father had to expose and deal with those issues before the man could rightly seek Him and hear His voice.

God wants us to get to know the language of His heart for us. When we lay down the preconceived notions about how He loves and feels toward us, we are more open to the things He wants to say about and to us in our quiet time with Him. Often, just a few words from Him directly to us will speak volumes.

RETREAT TIME

One of the most important tools for me in developing a listening lifestyle has been taking retreat times. This is simply a number of hours or days, away from responsibility and distraction, when I can spend time with God. Nearly all of the medium-to-large decisions in my life during the last decade have been made after seeking God during a retreat time.

Daily devotional time always has time constraints, so often it's hard to go deep in study or get into prolonged listening. I find that taking a Saturday morning at least a couple times a month to spend a few hours with my Father is essential to deepening our relationship. During that time, often I slow down and spend more time reading the Word, and I lay out everything that concerns me and ask Him to speak and guide. And He has countless times.

A few times a year, I try to take a whole weekend or even a week to do these things. Sometimes I'll do a fast, either from everything except liquid or maybe from certain types of foods or drinks with caffeine.

If you are in a relationship, you probably get a limited amount of daily time with your significant other. You can't wait for that date night or, if you are married, that weekend away. Simply think of your relationship with God like a romance, and retreat time becomes incredibly logical. Starve the time you spend with the one you love, and your relationship will suffer; spend special time together, and it will grow.

Like many other practices that come from a spiritual heritage, retreat time has great benefits for your creativity as well.

My friend Jeff Sparks, founder of the Heartland Film Festival, regularly takes a Friday off to retreat, pray, and seek God on things about the festival and its many ventures in the film industry. Jeff's consistent pursuit of God's guidance and will has spawned many visionary ideas and has been the foundation that's enabled the festival to positively influence the film industry for more than 15 years. They've been able to award more prize money to filmmakers than any other festival in the United States. (Check out Heartlandfilmfestival. org.)

Bill Gates, founder of Microsoft, was known to take a week-long retreat every year that he was with the company to clear his head and dream up new ideas. What he did during those retreats affected the world of technology for decades and into the future.

Your retreat times will affect your life and those around you for eternity.

God wants to talk with you.

Don't be afraid;

it's a good thing.

CHAPTER 7

HINDRANCES TO HEARING

The obedience that comes out of listening to God puts us securely in our truest vocation. It is a radical place to be—a place of freedom from the words of the world, the flesh, and the devil. No longer slaves to sin, but alive to God's voice, we are brought into that spacious place of genuine creativity.

—Leanne Payne

THERE ARE MANY HINDRANCES TO HEARING THE VOICE of the Holy Spirit, but it should be noted that encompassed in the sovereignty of God is the glorious truth that He can speak to us no matter what kind of shape or attitude we are in. These times of spontaneous and unexpected blessing when we are in a bad space or backslidden are wonderful mercies and should be enjoyed. Still, they are often a call to go deeper in our relationship with Him. Even on the human level, there are moments of surprise in relationships, moments of unexpected joy. But if the relationship is to be maintained and deepened, we have to make a choice to pursue it, often at the expense of something else. The more we learn about what delights the other person, and vice versa, the more intimate and sweet the relationship becomes. If we rely only on the moments of surprise and emotion, the relationship cannot grow or thrive.

MINIMIZING VOICES

The deeper we go, the more we realize that the call to be "in the world but not of it" is a colossal struggle. At the beginning of a Christian walk, it may seem that just knowing Who has saved you is enough. And often it is, but there is a point where the challenge of walking out a sanctified life becomes clear, and we are faced with arrested growth or the pain of going to the next level. And this is where we rediscover that so many attitudes in the world, upon close, honest analysis, are directly opposed to God's heart. We can expect the unsaved to pursue these attitudes with no recognition of their opposition to God, but Christians who continue to embrace unscriptural attitudes without their conscience being pricked probably are not hearing the voice of the Spirit. To consistently hear the Holy Spirit and sense God's heart, we must purify our hearts. Jesus said, "Blessed are the pure in heart, for they will see God" (Matt. 5:8). I believe He was speaking not only about seeing God in Heaven, but also about seeing the essence of God, the heart and desires of God, in daily life.

I've found that when I get some things in order in my life, eliminate distractions, and set my attitudes right, I have a better chance of hearing God's voice.

THE VOICE OF THE CULTURE

As creative people, we often crave stimulation, new ideas, and expressive voices. This is a good thing. Unfortunately, our culture has elevated these things—especially in the form of entertainment—beyond usefulness to idolatry. Instead of being part of the creation to enjoy in moderation, pleasure and entertainment as the means to ease our pain has become normal. What we consume may not cause us to fall away or sin immediately upon consumption, but because it's a product of the world and its philosophies, it is at odds with and in rebellion against God. It can become a nagging voice inside that squelches the voice of the Holy Spirit. It can promote subtle disillusionment that, gone unchecked, will develop into sin. "Each one is tempted when, by his own evil desire, he is dragged away and enticed. Then, after desire has conceived, it gives birth to sin; and sin, when it is full-grown, gives birth to death" (James 1:14-15).

I had an alternate career for eight years as a film reviewer for radio, TV, and print that required me to view nearly every movie that was released from 1988–1996. I saw thousands of things that were fundamentally opposed to the lifestyle of a follower of Christ, but I was able to rationalize that it was OK. *I'm saved and I know the truth*, I told myself, *so these philosophies and ideas can't really affect me*. But I grew more tolerant of violence, profanity, and sexuality, often looking forward to the thrill that viewing those things gave. The images and stories I was consuming often spilled over into my quiet time, causing my mind to wander constantly. Movies became an addiction as I searched for films that would give me that transcendent experience.

But I was puzzled: even though I'd been a Christian for many years, there was a persistent hollowness in my life. Oddly, that hollowness seemed to get stronger after a night out at the movies. I never imagined that it might be the echo of God's voice calling me to a deeper relationship with Him.

Later, I gave up reviewing films, cut back on the entertainment I was consuming, and turned toward my Father. My withered spiritual life blossomed, and I began to hear the voice of the Holy Spirit more clearly. Steve Turner says:

> We can't let our spirits take any amount of punishment and expect to remain unscathed. Sometimes we give ourselves permission to watch, listen or read such material because we say it's "just for a laugh" or "a bit of fun." But that usually means that our critical faculties are relaxed, and it is precisely at these times that our thinking can be shaped by ideas that are antagonistic toward faithful living. I think that T.S. Eliot had it right when he concluded, "It is just the literature that we read for 'amusement' or 'purely for pleasure' that may have the greatest influence upon us. It is the literature that we read with the least effort that can have the easiest and most insidious influence upon us."[1]

Recognizing and minimizing the distractions of the culture not only allows us to hear the Holy Spirit more easily, but it also allows creativity to flow. Julia Cameron says:

> It is a paradox that by emptying our lives of distractions we are actually filling up the well. Without distractions, we are once again thrust into the sensory world. With no newspaper to shield us, a train becomes a viewing gallery. With no novel to sink into (and no television to numb us out) an evening becomes a vast savanna in which furniture—and other assumptions—get rearranged.[2]

If you want to consistently know the joy of collaborating with God in the core of your being, hearing His voice and responding, you *must* judge and filter what you take in. And you have to do it in humility.

THE VOICE OF PRIDE

This leads us to a more subtle and consistently more insidious voice that can hinder us in hearing—the voice of pride. When we start to get a glimpse of what is wrong and right, pride can enter in and tell us we "got it." Sometimes we can take the concept of judging too far, into the arena of condemnation.

Our preconceived notions take the place of listening to God because we think we know what is happening or what should happen in our lives or circumstances. Dallas Willard says:

> In seeking and receiving God's word to us, therefore, we must at the same time seek and receive the

grace of humility. God will gladly give it to us if, trusting and waiting on him to act, we refrain from *pretending* we are what we know we are not, from *presuming* a favorable position for ourselves in any respect and from pushing or trying to override the will of others in our context. (This is a fail-safe recipe for humility.)[3]

Pride usually brings its friend rationalization along with it. An example of this from my life is the concept of self-promotion that I bought into for a number of years. I believed I needed to actively promote myself, because if my career and pursuits were going well and gaining ground, I would be better able to provide for my family. Therefore, I felt that the extra time and effort it took to promote myself (because I had so much to offer, right?) was actually an investment in my family. The fact that it made me feel good about the gifts God had given me was just gravy. My family didn't see it that way. They felt the truth was that I was just not there, and my pursuits were in fact selfish ego gratification.

My rationalization was a result of the prideful belief that I could and should control my own path and then assume that God would be with me. The reality for the Christian is that the Father leads us where He wants us when we seek Him and that we can trust Him to provide for us and promote us as we are faithful with what He has given and obedient to follow His direction. There is certainly a place for stepping out, moving forward, taking chances, risking failure, bringing innovation, and the like, but it must all be done on the foundation of a vibrant, seeking, daily relationship with the Father.

A good example of my out-of-control pride and rationalization came after the local paper asked to do a Valentine's-weekend story on how my wife (at the time) and I had met. I saw it as a big step into new areas in my career as a film reviewer, and of course, my success would be great for the family. I asked my wife to wear certain clothes and to clean up the basement, an area of the house that we struggled with, so that I could give a charming tour to the writer. When my wife balked at these things, I became insistent, believing that she didn't understand the importance of pursuing success. My harsh and prideful treatment of her was one of the last straws in our marriage, and by the time the cute story with the big color picture came out in the Sunday paper, I no longer cared about the success of my reviewing career.

Madeleine L'Engle says that our pride can hinder creativity by keeping us from going into new areas in collaboration with Him: "We all tend to make zealous judgments and thereby close ourselves off from revelation. If we feel that we already know something in its totality, then we fail to keep our ears and eyes open to that which may expand or even change that which we so zealously think we know."[4]

Pride is incredibly subtle and often concealed to those afflicted by it. It can be identified and stopped by daily seeking the Father's face through prayer, reading the Word, and the input of honest, loving people. "For the word of God is living and active. Sharper than any double-edged sword, it penetrates even to dividing soul and spirit, joints and marrow; it judges the thoughts and attitudes of the heart"

(Heb. 4:12). "Wounds from a friend can be trusted, but an enemy multiplies kisses" (Prov. 27:6).

As a sensitive, creative person who may be susceptible to insecurities, you *must* search for pride and identify it in your life, praying as David did, "Search me, O God, and know my heart; test me and know my anxious thoughts. See if there is any offensive way in me, and lead me in the way everlasting" (Ps. 139:23-24). Pride can send your life in the wrong direction and cause you to live a lie; it will frustrate God's plan for you and hurt those you love. Rest assured, the luxury of letting pride live in you *will* bring you down. "Pride goes before destruction; a haughty spirit before a fall" (Prov. 16:18). "A man's pride brings him low, but a man of lowly spirit gains honor" (Prov. 29:23). "…God will bring down their pride, despite the cleverness of their hands" (Isa. 25:11).

OUR OWN VOICE

All this takes us into a most delicate area—the area of our own voice as a hindrance to hearing the Holy Spirit. I believe it's God's plan that our voice (who He made us) and His spirit can and should become partners in life and the creative process, that as we grow we learn to defer to the Holy Spirit without losing a sense of who we are. In fact, as we defer and seek God's will, He will show us more clearly who we really are, as opposed to who we think we are. This is truly one of the sweetest revelations of the deep Christian walk.

A phenomenon that has swept our country in the last 50 years is the emphasis on self-esteem. This became a trend around the same time that true, committed Christianity was being watered down, becoming more of a label than a lifestyle. Exalting self-esteem is the humanistic way of man attaching value to himself, a craving that is placed in us by God for Him to fulfill. If we're no longer in contact with God, we take it upon ourselves to fill that craving. In order for this to work, we must elevate our will and dreams above the will of God, making it unnecessary to seek God. This attitude shows up in Christians when we ask God to bless our decisions instead of seeking His desires for us. As Christians, and especially creative people, we must "get it" that *God* knows better than we do how our lives and projects should go and that if we seek Him, He will share the information.

This includes the areas of dreams for our life. Often, God does put a dream into our hearts, but then we take over and try to work it out. This has led to thousands of years of trouble. Think of Abraham, who received the dream of fathering many nations with his wife, Sarah, but took it into his own hands and had a child with her servant, setting off several thousand years of conflict between Arabs and Jews. Or look at evangelist Jim Bakker, whose dream of reaching multitudes for Christ and providing Christians with teaching and encouragement got wildly off track and turned criminal. Or think of the times you got ahead of God and ended up with a big mess on your hands. Isaiah 50:11 has something to say about running ahead of God with our dreams: "But now, all you who light fires and provide yourselves with flaming torches, go, walk in the light of your fires and of the torches you have set ablaze. This is what you shall receive from my hand: You will lie down in torment."

Sometimes a dream comes from our own imagination, but we cling to it because we have allowed it to define us. After years of trying to make it happen, we may be overwhelmed with frustration and hopelessness, until we finally understand the meaning of Isaiah 55:8, "For my thoughts are not your thoughts, neither are my ways your ways...." That leaves us helpless and powerless; right where our Father wants us. Walking down the path of fulfilling our own dreams and plans can sometimes bring a level of happiness, but it will never compare to the joy and fulfillment of walking daily in the presence and will of God.

To say that all creative ideas come from God is, in fact, partially true. He constructed our brains and our thought processes and gave us the ability to think creatively. That is a gift from Him to us. But in the sense that specific ideas should automatically be assumed to be gifts from God, even in the context of the Christian artist, is mistaken. It is this notion that Christian artists, just on the basis that they are Christians, can assume that all creative ideas they get are from God that has led to much bad work, depression, disillusionment, and crises of faith.

There are a million ideas out there, many of them good. What we want *now* is to pursue the ideas that God wants us to pursue during our moment in time. Handing over our small-focus and naturally-based logic makes it possible for us to fulfill our life purpose as we search for and rely on His larger, omniscience-based logic.

A thought from Leanne Payne balances out this section:

Do not be afraid that what you are hearing is "Just me." You need to know what "just me," your deep heart, knows. Within a short time you will be able to discern the difference between the knowledge you already have—the wisdom already given you and a part of your heart—and the word God speaks to you afresh. Both are important and needful.

She goes on to say that you should not overanalyze a word you receive, but look back after a while and reread it. It should become clear. "And the more experience you gain in prayer, the easier it will be to identify if it is you or God speaking."[5]

IMMORALITY

During the Clinton intern scandal, a famous actor (and Clinton supporter) was quoted as saying that we should expect and accept this type of behavior because, "He is a powerful man and powerful men have powerful libidos." Politicians and artists have operated this way for centuries. It is a fact that people who flow in creativity often feel things more strongly than those who are less creative. The larger fact is that our God is big enough to meet us where we are. When we are honest with Him and others about the things we struggle with, that honesty serves to defuse the power and loosen the grip that those things have on us.

The human body is certainly one of the most beautiful things God has created. It's amazing to think that He even created specific parts of our bodies for pleasure, pleasure to be shared with another person—in marriage. As artists, we intuitively know the importance and the beauty of this union. We understand the spark, affirmation, possibility, and connectedness sexual union can bring. We crave these things maybe more than the act itself. For this reason, we may be susceptible to temptations in this area, and that is why it's important to remind ourselves and each other of God's view on this.

Of course, God's view is contrary to the world's view, which says sex is a right and a legitimate part of any relationship with the opposite gender. Paul says that it is much more: "Do you not know that your bodies are members of Christ Himself? Shall I then take the members of Christ and unite them with a prostitute? Never! Do you not know that he who unites himself with a prostitute is one with her in body? For it is said, 'The two will become one flesh'" (1 Cor. 6:15-16). Louis Smedes brings this home in *Sex for Christians*:

> It does not matter what the two people (who are having sex) have in mind…The reality of the act, unfelt and unnoticed by them, is this: It unites them—body and soul—to each other. It unites them in that strange, impossible to pinpoint sense of "one flesh." There is no such thing as casual sex, no matter how casual people are about it. The Christian assaults reality in his night out at the brothel. He uses a woman and puts her back in a closet where she can be forgotten; but the reality is that he has put away a person with whom he has done something that was meant to inseparably join them. This is what is at stake for Paul in the question of sexual intercourse between unmarried people.[6]

When we engage in sex outside of marriage, we do damage to the other person, ourselves, and our relationship with God. We may lose a piece of ourselves that we gave in the bonding with another, and we may develop emotional scars when we break that bond, scars that can create barriers when we finally do bond with our mate. We give satan a foothold to torment us with memories, and we cloud our relationship with God. Incredibly, God often heals these things. Or sometimes we may have to live with the consequences. Either way, a sexual slip will probably cause a setback for you.

Of course, you don't have to go as far as having illicit sex to feel the effects of lust and sexual sin. Purity can be a difficult path to walk in our culture, especially when many of the artists around us are totally immersed in the pursuit of sexual pleasure. But we must strive for purity if we want the consistent guidance and communication of the Holy Spirit in our work. This may require a huge effort on our part, which could include reducing or even abstaining from dating, making a conscious effort to discontinue flirting or suggestive joking, becoming consistently accountable to someone or a group, and getting more involved in a vibrant church. It may require watching fewer movies and less television, or even switching channels when the soap commercial comes on. It's all worth it because Jesus said, "Blessed are the pure in heart, for they will see God" (Matt. 5:8). He is talking about now—about seeing the nature of God, seeing what God is doing, and seeing what He wants us to do.

A classic example of how a prominent person has approached purity is Billy Graham's policy. Throughout his ministry, Graham always traveled with a group of men he was accountable to, and he was never alone in a room with a woman other than his wife. We all know the names of other ministers who were once of Graham's stature whose ministries were tainted because they never set up such a system. In *Rock and Roll Rebellion*, Mark Joseph suggests the concept of Christian musicians hiring a "road pastor" to give band members someone to talk to while they're away from home. "Certainly taking a pastor on the road will be an added expense for the artist and the label, but in the long run it will be money saved by avoiding things that have traditionally plagued rock stars on the road: affairs, paternity suits, family breakups, trashed hotel rooms, drug problems, and so on."[7]

These things do happen to Christian artists. Joseph also suggests that a road pastor could be a reality checker, "to remind the artists—in the midst of thousands of adoring fans—that they are not to be worshipped, that they are messengers of God and not gods." Not only that, but the road pastor could also provide much-needed spiritual strength while the artist is away from home and enduring what is often a very draining schedule.

At the time that I interviewed singer Dan Haseltine of Jars of Clay, that group had two people who served in the role of road pastors. One dealt more on an individual, relational level. "He'll come out on the road on tour and we'll go have coffee with him," Dan said, "and he'll just kind of talk to us and ask us a lot of challenging questions." The other one was very seasoned, having gone out with bands like Stryper and DC Talk. "We call him the fountain of Scripture because he usually speaks Scripture constantly. He's the one who keeps us pushing in on our relationships in the band. We call our road pastors our perspective counselors. Basically, they bring us down to earth … and hold us accountable."

If you have fallen into sexual sin or had sexual activity in the past that still haunts you, call on God's marvelous grace. That grace is "unfair," bringing forgiveness, healing, and a fresh start to those who don't deserve it. "If we confess our sins, He is faithful and just and will forgive us our sins and purify us from all unrighteousness" (1 John 1:9). Some good-old-fashioned thorough repentance will go a long way to clearing up the guilt, shame, or other effects of sin you may be feeling.

There are many resources for dealing with sexual sin and immorality, but some of the best are Stephen Arterburn's books *Every Man's Battle* and *Every Woman's Battle*. I recommend them if this is a difficult issue for you.

THE VOICE OF THE ENEMY

For some, the risk of actually hearing the devil when we are trying to hear God is too much to handle. What if satan tells us a lie and we believe it and mess everything up? God provides protection against that. Remember, regardless of what the horror movies say, God is far greater than the devil. Satan is only a finite, created being; God is the infinite, uncreated, multiple "omni" being. And He has given us the power to stand against our enemy.

The fear that satan will slip in and lie to us while we're listening to God is just another one of satan's cunning tactics.

Certainly, it is possible, but we deal with it with the weapons God has given us; I'll say more about that in a moment. Dallas Willard adds some perspective to this subject, saying, "It would be strange if we came to shun the genuine simply because it resembled the counterfeit."[8]

Still, we must be aware of the devil's schemes. I'm certain that he and his minions influence many of the things we've talked about—worldly attitudes, pride, immorality. But satan is often more subtle than we give him credit for. I've heard it said and believe it is true that satan speaks to us in a voice that sounds like our own. We must discern the difference between his, ours, and God's voices by knowing the Word and applying it, by resisting satan, and by asking God to speak and fight for us. The devil is a ferocious-sounding enemy (as a roaring lion); he often uses theatrics and deception to play us to the point where we hurt ourselves.

During World War II, Winston Churchill organized the allies in a policy of deception to defeat the Germans. At some point in the war, the Polish Secret Police captured from a sinking U-boat a German code-writing machine called Enigma and gave it to the British. The Germans didn't know this, but it probably wouldn't have concerned them much, because the code was considered uncrackable. By a miracle, the Brits *did* crack the code and succeeded in capturing every German operative in England, replacing them with their own people and sending tainted information to the enemy. But in order for the deception to work, they had to mix accurate information with the false.

The defining moment of this deception came on D-Day. Hitler had a *preconceived notion* that the allies would land at the Port of Calais because it was the easiest access and the closest to England, so all the fake information that was sent to him over the spy network pointed in that direction. It fed his preconception. The Allies took the deception as far as building thousands of fake ships and troops to float off the coast of Calais. Without this deception, the Allied landing at Normandy could never have been a success. The Germans massed a large part of their defenses in the wrong place.

This example gives some insight into how deception works and how the master deceiver may work it. First, note the mixture of accurate and tainted information. This is often called "worldly wisdom"; it has roots in or the appearance of truth because it is often based on experience, however limited. Only the Holy Spirit can lead us into discerning what is truth and what is a lie. Second, Satan uses our preconceived notions to set us in the wrong direction and reinforces them to keep us going that way. He can even use the preconceived notions that may kick in after we get direction from the Lord. That is a key reason to be in constant, daily contact and communication with the Father and to be always seeking His will. Steve Turner says:

> I'm convinced that the world of the arts, media, and entertainment, because of its access to the imaginations of so many millions, is a place of great interest to the spiritual forces of evil. As a movie director recently observed, "L.A. is the town that controls world storytelling for both children and adults.'" Artists have no special protection. In

fact, because of their tendency to be curious about all forms of experience and their need to avoid rigid forms of thinking, they are probably more vulnerable to temptation. The standard protection kit offered to all Christians is the belt of truth, the breastplate of righteousness, the shoes of readiness, the shield of faith, the helmet of salvation, the sword of the Spirit and prayer (Ephesians 6). We can't survive with the T-Shirt of Sunday school memories and the baseball cap of personal vision.[9]

Many Christians know little about the armor of God and resisting the devil. I encourage you to make prayers along these lines a daily part of your routine. I actually go through the motions of putting the armor on in order to bring it to life for me. It only takes a few seconds, and if someone sees you, just act like you're working on your hip-hop moves.

DEALING WITH SINFUL ATTITUDES AND UNFORGIVENESS

I talked about this earlier, but it's certainly worth mentioning again.

Peter said that the way we treat people has the potential to be a hindrance to communication with God. "Husbands, in the same way be considerate as you live with your wives, and treat them with respect as the weaker partner and as heirs with you of the gracious gift of life, so that nothing will hinder your prayers" (1 Pet. 3:7). It's bit of a mystery how this works, but the concept is a great motivator for me to hang in there and work through issues with my wife.

Jesus said that unforgiveness can hinder our relationship with God. "And when you stand praying, if you hold anything against anyone, forgive him, so that your Father in heaven may forgive you your sins" (Mark 11:25). He also made it a part of His model prayer for us: "Forgive us our debts, as we also have forgiven our debtors" (Matt. 6:12). Practicing forgiveness is an essential, daily part of our walk if we want to be hearing from the Holy Spirit. It is often not just a one-time thing. If you've been hurt by someone over a period of time that may have even resulted in a horribly abusive situation for you—maybe even a situation that is ongoing—it is essential to practice forgiveness. That may just be turning your will and your heart toward forgiveness even when you don't feel like it and asking God to meet you there, to change your heart even when it seems you have a *right* to your unforgiveness. *Not* doing this is at odds with God's heart and a sure way to hinder yourself from hearing the Holy Spirit.

Sometimes the first step toward forgiveness, even if you're not yet willing to forgive, is to be willing to be willing. Sounds like psychobabble, but it's really just handing our fragile and hurt will over to God.

OVERCOMING HINDRANCES

There are ways to deal with every hindrance to hearing God's voice that might be thrown at us. "No temptation has seized you except what is common to man. And God is faithful; He will not let you be tempted beyond what you can bear. But when you are tempted, He will also provide a way out so that you can stand up under it" (1 Cor. 10:13).

God knows each of our vulnerable points, and as we recognize and get honest about them and seek His face, He will show us how to avoid them.

I'll wrap up this section with a thought from Leanne Payne, stated in her uniquely intellectual, authentic, and wise way:

> Listening Prayer (a listening lifestyle) is a vital facet of God's presence with us. It is a place of freedom from the voices of the world, the flesh, and the devil. Those latter voices, when harkened to and obeyed, pull us toward nonbeing and death. To fail to listen to God is to be listening to one or another (or all) of those voices. It is to miss the vital walk in the Spirit and our immensely creative collaboration with Him. This collaboration requires the new self—one in union with Christ—that is always maturing in Him.[10]

Relax.

God wants you to know His voice.

He is your Shepherd, and you are His sheep.

He will lead you in the true ways of knowing and hearing Him as you come to Him daily

with all you have.

Then hearing and obeying His voice

will build a foundation for finding divine inspiration

in all areas of your life.

CHAPTER 8

PERSONAL EXAMPLES
OF TRUE COLLABORATION

...When the words mean even more than the writer knew they meant, then the writer has been listening. And sometimes when we listen, we are led into places we do not expect, into adventures we do not always understand.

—Madeleine L'Engle[1]

A S I SAID EARLIER, I'VE SPENT MANY YEARS pursuing creative expression. I felt that, if I could bring out who I am and what I feel, God would bless it. Sometimes He did; most of the time it was a struggle. It's not that the presence of a struggle means that God is not with you; often He uses struggles to refine, test, and bless us. But I rarely really *knew* that God was totally involved and guiding my projects. Much of the motivation for what I did was pride, although I didn't know it. I thought I was believing in and fighting for myself.

Then, in January 1996, my marriage disintegrated. God had been calling me to look at several areas in my life, and suddenly I could no longer put it off. I sought Him with everything I had and found, as I started to really listen to Him, that He was speaking. The small steps taken in obedience to His voice built into larger ones, and the confirmations of hearing His voice built into a new listening lifestyle. Manipulation and control fell off like broken shackles, and pride was identified and made the subject of a daily "deliver me" prayer. Struggles with these issues still continue, but they have nowhere near the hold they once did.

The refocus on God and overhaul of my attitudes, plus the emotional turmoil of my situation, took all my energy during this time, so I effectively stopped all creative pursuits except what was necessary to keep up my position as a radio station production director. In addition to the redirection of energy, I stopped these pursuits because I didn't want to go down any more of my own roads, roads that had taken me further into pride and away from my family. I was frightened that I'd never be creative again, that I was saying good-bye to a part of myself, but I felt it a small price to pay to know that I was seeking God and was truly in His will. This season lasted about a year. I gave up my weekly sideline as a film critic for television and radio, laid aside the video and film projects I was working toward, and pretty much quit writing anything except lengthy journal entries. The creativity required in my job was often a stretch or even a burden.

Then God started drawing me back. But this time I consulted Him and invited His Holy Spirit to give specific direction, just like I had been learning to do in my everyday life. And He came near and started to partner with me. It's been a wonderful journey; one that, after more than a decade, I still feel like I'm just beginning.

The first experience with this that I had was while working on a highly-produced promotional announcement for Alanis Morrisette with music, voice, and sound effects. Trying to hear the Spirit's leading, I felt a check on a music clip I had put in, so I waited. After a short time, I felt I should look for a new clip and read a lyric sheet until I came across some lyrics that really fit. The witness of the Spirit was there—I felt a "yes" inside—and the new clip fit perfectly. It drew the promo together in a powerful way. That project went on to win the state award for best radio promotional announcement of that year. I had won awards before, but I knew that this one was a gift. I was fully aware of God's partnership in my work, and this was humbling—not an ego-inflating kudo, but a "postcard from God" to let me know that He was there and interested in my work. He was interested in working with me! The work didn't need to define me or prop me up. *God* was defining me, communing with me, and showing His love.

There was one night, actually during the time when I had laid everything down, when I came home and felt compelled by the Spirit to write some songs to express the things I was going through. I had always wanted to write songs, but I'm not a musician. I asked for His guidance and partnership, and soon a song came that felt like it was directly from Heaven. It worked and expressed exactly where I was. I cried when I sang it. It was a gift. I took it as something personal, maybe never to be shared with anyone but my daughter, and stored it away in my journal.

Sometime after that, our church, the Indianapolis Vineyard, began two small groups, one for the arts and one for songwriting. I was drawn to both, but felt I should go to the arts group. Over the weeks, we began to prepare projects for the Christmas season. Our pastor asked us to work up something for Advent along the lines of waiting on God. As we talked and prayed, a plan started to develop. One evening we got together and waited on God in prayer. He led us in a direction that was brought to life by painting large panels with images of saints who had waited for God. One side showed them in the waiting posture; dark and bowed down. The other showed the receiving of the promises. The dark-sided panels were hung at the same time and then turned over one by one each week as the stories were told at midweek services. We'd seen something like this done by an artist named Kyle Ragsdale.

The services were powerful, but the presence of the paintings took them to another level. Tears, cleansing, and blessings were abundant the whole month, and it was clear God was doing something to bring the arts to life, to bring the arts to a real place of expressing Him to us. This was pivotal, because the Father truly revealed how He could use this expression to affirm us and speak to us in our church, if we would take the time to really include Him in the process.

Later, I also joined the songwriters' group, and after a few months I shared the song God had given me. I was nervous as I sang it a cappella. It was hard to swallow some of the criticism the group freely handed out, but I knew the Father had led me to share the song. A few months later, the group was planning to sing their songs at the monthly church coffeehouse. The leader asked me to do the song, and one of the musicians volunteered to accompany with guitar. It was such a real blessing to see this coming to life.

But the night of the coffeehouse was another turning point. I prayed for the Holy Spirit's anointing and truly gave the whole experience to Him. I was relaxed and carefree, an unusual experience for me, and the performance was pure pleasure. It was alive and real, just like the lyrics God had given, and the audience received it well. I was naturally humbled by what He had done. I felt no need to build on it later, to try to follow it up or to make sure that the right people were sufficiently impressed. None of that mattered. God had put it all together, and for the first time, natural humility flowed out when compliments were given.

We hear, as Christians, that God will develop us. For me, the key to that is obedience, doing the small things, the things out of our comfort zone, that the Father prompts us to do. As I said, I had never written a coherent song. I'd never sung solo in front of an audience, but He gave the opportunities and over time showed that it was His plan. And in obeying Him, I discovered He was trying to show me more of who He made me as a creative person.

A note here: one thing to watch is that, after getting a revelation or direction from the Father, we should not stop listening. We have a tendency to "get it and go." Instead, what needs to happen is daily, consistent consulting and listening to the Spirit's desire. Songwriting or painting, even my current job, could just be blips on the screen of His plan for me. If I want to own it, to let it define me, to become it, then I get back to providing for myself and not trusting in God. It's like saying, "Thanks for getting me this far; You are really good. I think I can take it from here." It's another step in our faith to be able to take, absorb, and really feel the blessing or the leading and then give it back, realizing that the journey continues, the leading still is just as desperately needed, and true servanthood is being open to joyfully go and do whatever He leads. The more you do this, the more joy comes in the doing. It's not all joy; the denial of the flesh and the comfort it perpetually seeks is painful, sometimes overwhelmingly so. But the joy of knowing that you are not holding back, that the Father can and will use you, is pure and comforting.

These partnership successes are relatively small and personal, but they are significant; the development of an attitude or a habit starts with small things. In one of His parables, Jesus promises, "You have been faithful in a few things, I will put you in charge of many things" (Matt. 25:21).

The next example came during a long and difficult creative process lasting five months. At the radio station, one of my responsibilities is to develop the script, soundtrack, and fireworks choreography for an annual Labor Day fireworks show we do that is precisely synchronized to music. When it works, it is one of the most amazing things you'll ever see, a half hour of fireworks exploding to beats, crescendos, and descriptive words or attitudes in the songs. Around four hundred thousand people come to the banks of the White River to watch the show, and another quarter of a million watch the simulcast on television. The pressure is on!

I asked for the Holy Spirit's partnership and felt a leading to go with a theme I had toyed with: movie music. My peers and bosses at the station received it with ambivalence, but they didn't have anything better. As I waded through all the material available, movie soundtracks, clips and quotes, I came to a point of being overwhelmed. This was a monumental job!

One night I decided to stay late until the Holy Spirit gave me some real direction. He did, and the outline of the show was set that night. A weight was lifted—until my boss started picking the show apart. Hope disintegrated. Two months of darkness followed; squabbles about elements, direction, and tone continued. A change in theme was even brought up. I kept referring back to the original outline for guidance, worked out compromises on elements, and waited for guidance on specific problems. It came down to the point that my boss said it wasn't working and that next year he wouldn't listen to my theme ideas. Devastating.

I continued to pray and have others pray, and a few things started to come together. As we went through the tedious process of plotting the fireworks choreography (what points in the songs we wanted to hit; the exact time each firework needed to be launched to hit those points; how long it should stay in the sky; as well as what style, size, and color it should be), it became apparent that this was a good show. If it worked, it could be the best in our 16-year history. My boss became more confident as he saw it too.

The night of the show, I was relaxed; it was in God's hands. I picked a spot away from the command center to really see and enjoy it. It was beautiful, nearly perfect in mood and execution, with the fireworks hitting at the precise times. The crowd roared. I knew it was my Father's direct gift when I saw it. He was partnering with me and the efforts of our team. It was affirmation; it was love; it was ecstasy.

I had prayed that the Holy Spirit would speak through the entire show, that He would reveal Himself to the audience, and I believe He did. The comments were overwhelming. The CEO of the company couldn't stop trying to express his excitement afterward, the overwhelming response was amazement, and the consensus was that the show was the best ever. Even the founder of the show, who had done it for 13 years before me, was blown away when he saw the videotape. My boss apologized and agreed that it was a phenomenal show.

I believe that my Father showed a little of Himself to nearly three-quarters of a million people that night, and the knowledge that He *chose* to involve me in that process is real and gratifying. This is the kind of real, authentic, palpable partnership with the One who made me that I want to be the hallmark of my life and creative pursuits.

My next example turned out to be a symphony of collaboration with the Holy Spirit as I took time to pray through every element. In October 2000, the church asked me to design and organize some Advent services for December. I took a couple of weeks to pray about it and then felt God's blessing. As I asked Him about the themes of the services, He seemed to be speaking about the concept of experiencing an intimate time with Him, of being gentle and childlike, of presenting our precious gifts to Him, turning the Advent theme around to make it giving from us to Him. I was inspired to use as many areas of the arts as we could—spoken word, painting, dance, song, and audience interaction.

As I prayed one day, I was reminded of a reference book I had picked up at a Christian bookstore called *Music and the Arts in Christian Worship*.[2] It normally was very expensive but had been marked down 70 percent. I had felt led to buy it, and now I found that it had a wealth of wisdom and guidance about working the arts into a service. I journaled that I felt ready to explode, and I had a couple of nights with so many ideas and thoughts flowing through my mind that it was hard to want to sleep. I was having a blast creating and visualizing with the inspiration of the Holy Spirit.

One day as I prayed about the project and read Psalm 80, God gave me a short and sweet song based on that chapter to add into the service. I shared it with our worship leader, and she put music to it and sang it. It was perfect on the night of the service, and it was so exciting to see something go from Holy Spirit inspiration to full performance in a short period of time.

I started praying about artists to paint some paintings for the service, and God led me to two women in our church. There were many wonderful confirmations and nudges as we prayed about what to paint, and I wrote in my journal, "I'm thoroughly enjoying the productivity and preparation." We got together on a Saturday night, prayed over each other and anointed our canvases with oil, and then started painting the visuals that God had given us. The vivid colors we used almost seemed too loud, until we put the three paintings together and marveled at the balance and how they complimented one another. It was apparent that God had orchestrated the theme, colors, and composition of each painting, just as we had asked!

Dance also was worked into the program, and our dancer picked "Welcome to Our World" to interpret. Her interpretation was inspired and anointed, and people came up afterward to say how it really affected them.

God led me to choose some readers and speakers, all with cool confirmations, one of whom was so overcome by the presence of the Spirit that night that he could hardly go on.

A few months before I knew about this service, while at a Christian conference, I had received a visual of a bunch of priests breaking out in singing "Prepare Ye the Way of the Lord" from the musical *Godspell*. It turned out that a variation of that was perfect for the Advent service. We worked it in, and it was a joy to behold!

I felt led to ask a very talented musician in the church to come up with an original song for one of the services. He had an idea, but then he waffled back and forth, finally saying he wasn't in a good place and couldn't do it. A few days later, I prayed and felt clearly that I should ask him again. That day I went to the mall, asking God to guide my every step. I randomly ran into him at a store and encouraged him to change his mind. He came up with a version of "Little Drummer Boy" that incorporated his testimony. It was magical when he sang it, and the response was overwhelming and incredibly encouraging for him. The pastor asked him to sing it again at another service, and he recorded it and made a CD, which many people bought.

The three paintings we were led to make for those services were each four foot square: there was a road with a wild, swirling sky (loosely symbolizing hope), a huge heart with a cross embedded in it (symbolizing love), and a sort of psychedelic tree, sprouted from a mustard seed (symbolizing faith). We felt led to have the audience come up during the service to somehow give their precious gifts to God. After seeking God's inspiration, He gave us the idea to have them write the precious personal gift they would like to offer to God on a colored sticky note and then stick it on the heart painting! We made the sticky-note colors match the heart and created a whole new work of art with the audience's help. It was beautiful and definitely Holy Spirit inspired.

The day of the first service was tough; everything went wrong. I was confused and stressed as one thing after another happened. I had planned and organized the service but couldn't stay because it conflicted with a Christmas program my daughter was in at school. Here's what I journaled:

I hightailed it back to the church after Hailee's program and made the last few minutes of the service, collapsing in my seat and feeling different emotions.... Then something happened inside me as Communion was served. I had been praying that You would kill my pride, but nicely; that You'd release me of it. During Communion, You showed me that that's what all the hassles of the day were about. This was not mine, but Yours! Ours. And I couldn't do it. You set it up, and I'd have to organize it and leave that night. Go away! Like You were saying, "Thank you, son. Now, go!" And the hassles and frustrations let me know it was not in my control!!! I started laughing, giggling.

What a relief, what a lesson, what a sense of humor. You answered my prayer, taught me, and blessed people and Yourself at the same time! Afterward, when people told me how they liked it, I could only shrug and know that You had done it! Thank You for that sweet mercy! This was an excellent lesson to learn before next week's service, especially since I was speaking.

The second service was very smooth, with none of the troubles of the week before. I felt God's peace and anointing all day. When I went to write the message, I could feel the Holy Spirit was present and collaborating with me, and I was almost giddy with excitement. The message translated very well that night, and everyone "got" the concept of putting the note on the heart as a symbol of giving gifts to God.

Our pastor affirmed that the message was right on and even used the theme and call in his Sunday message.

So many answered prayers came in preparation for these Advent services! I wrote in my journal, "Now I have a glimmer of what the apostle John meant when he wrote that there were many other things that Jesus did and he supposed if they were all written down, all the books in the world couldn't contain them. You are *so* rich and show and do *so much* when I'm flowing and following you. And I'm reminded that so much of what You directed came during quiet time and specific prayer about the services. That would have not been known if that time had not been taken!"

Of course, it's impossible to box God in, expecting Him to work or speak the same way on every project. Often there will be little or no feeling of partnership with Him, only faith that it is happening because we asked for it.

A few years ago, I had an amazing example of this. Through my whole radio career, beginning as a teenager, I had always prayed two things: that God would speak through me and that He would give me divine, unmerited, supernatural favor with whomever heard my voice and whomever I worked with. I've seen a lot of fruit from these requests over the years but often wondered about what I didn't see. Looking back, I see that I was inviting God to partner with me years before He brought the concept of finding divine inspiration through collaborating with God to life, but the listening part of the equation was severely lacking.

In the 1980s, I spent three years at WCFL Chicago, a legendary AM station that went with a Christian format for a few years. I was often on at night, a time when the station's powerful signal could be heard thousands of miles away, up into Canada and all across the eastern United States. I once got a tape of my voice from someone who had picked us up in Finland! I knew it was possible for millions of people to hear us but had heard few life-changing testimonies.

That time in my life was also full of personal struggle. My young marriage was not going well, and it weighed on my mind on those nights on the air. Years later I sometimes wondered if anything really good had happened during that time in Chicago Christian radio; the whole period seemed like a bad dream because of the personal turmoil that went on. Then, a few years ago I went to a creativity retreat at a suburban Indianapolis church. At the end of an enjoyable weekend, everyone gave his or her e-mail address to the facilitator. When I gave my name, one of the other participants, Danny Wright, looked startled and said, "There was a Scott McElroy on the radio in Chicago in the '80s." I told him that was me, and he exclaimed, "Dude, you changed my life!" He said he had been talking about me at conferences and to youth groups for many years!

When we met for lunch a week later, he laid out the whole story. He had been a struggling 15-year-old in the car with his parents very late one night on the way back from visiting his grandmother, who was dying in the hospital. His dad turned on the radio, looking for some Christian music, and came across WCFL. After a few minutes, I came on and said something very simple, and instantly, Danny said, God spoke to him, and he knew what he was supposed to do the rest of his life: youth ministry. I was broadcasting from Chicago, and this teenager and his family were listening in Virginia, hundreds of miles away. Danny did become a youth minister and told that story about the deejay in Chicago to youth groups in several states through the years, finally ending up in Indianapolis, where I happened to be living. We miraculously met 20 years after the fact, and it was a great grace to me that God would give a little glimpse into how He had answered those prayers to be used, even with the broken condition of my life. And I think it's a little flash of what Heaven will be like for all of us who pray to collaborate with God in what He is doing and believe in faith that He is working through us.

Before I end this chapter, here's a word about giving God the glory for these successes and remaining focused on Him in the middle of adulation. The most effective story I've ever heard about giving these things to God came from the late Corrie ten Boom. When someone asked her how she handled all the praise and positive comments that came to her after she would speak or be in public, she said that she would take each comment as if someone was handing her a beautiful flower—graciously and with thanks. Then at the end of the day, she would gather all the flowers in a bouquet and offer them up to God.

Perfect.

When you learn to listen and obey
God will build a surprisingly rich history
of collaboration with you.
You'll find that, as you collaborate with Him,
you'll discover more of your true self.
That discovery is a gift that only He can give.
He does this because He loves and values you
more than anyone you've ever known
and because it thrills Him to watch you
become who you were intended to be.
Collaboration with God can be
one of the most fulfilling experiences
in the universe.
For you and Him.

CHAPTER 9

CURRENT ARTISTS
ON DIVINE INSPIRATION

As THIS BOOK HAS TAKEN SHAPE, I've sought out a number of professional Christian artists who are active in music, theater, writing, and the visual arts to hear how they collaborate with the Holy Spirit in their creative process.

As you'll see, each artist has a different process. Some feel they hear God's direction more clearly, and others find it more mysterious.

Artists who are featured in this chapter are Thomas Blackshear, painter; Ron DiCianni painter; Dan Haseltine, musician, Jars of Clay; Peter Furler, musician, The Newsboys; Buzz McLaughlin, playwright and author; Gary Bayer, actor and director; and Walter Wangerin Jr., author.

I asked each person a series of similar questions:

"How does God work with you in your creative process?"

"How do you put yourself in a position to collaborate with God?"

"Could you share some specific examples of when you felt the Holy Spirit's collaboration with you?"

THOMAS BLACKSHEAR

Blackshear is an acclaimed artist and sculptor who has created some of the most recognizable spiritual images of recent decades. As an illustrator, he designed twenty postage stamps for the U.S. Postal Service. His powerful painting, "Forgiven," has affected thousands of people around the world.

Thomas's process starts with asking God to give Him an image to paint. He says he tries to let go of his preferences and do what God gives him to do, putting aside the feeling that he needs to top himself. I spoke to him by phone while he was at home in Colorado. Following is a transcript of our conversation.

Scott McElroy (SM): I hear that you sometimes fast and pray before working on a project.

Thomas Blackshear (TB): Yeah…sometimes I would pray and just get it [an idea] right away; sometimes I would pray and pray, and I'd have to go into fasting, and then I'd have to wait. And when it came, [I knew] it was the Lord because it was so powerful. A lot of people know me for "Forgiven," and that was one that I fasted and prayed about; that took some time before it came. I think I waited almost two and a half or three weeks before it came.

I remember the day it came, because it was a Wednesday-night prayer meeting, and there was going to be a worship service downstairs afterwards. They asked if anybody needed prayer for anything specific, so I said, "Yeah, I've got this painting I need to get done, and I really need someone to pray with me because I've fasted and prayed and I know God's going to give it to me, but so far nothing has happened." So they gathered around and laid hands on me and prayed, then I went downstairs to the worship service...and while I was in the middle of singing a song, He flashed the image in my head...and when I got it, I knew it! I said, *Whoa! This is powerful.* And I knew the name and everything!

The first time that ever happened to me I think was back in 1985. There was a show coming up in San Francisco, when I was living there, and I was supposed to put a painting in [to the show]. I had never done a painting for an art show, so I didn't know what to do. So I asked God. I prayed one day, and I said, "Lord, would You please give me a painting? I don't know what to do. If You don't mind, would You give me something that would be beautiful, with a nice composition, and powerful? Whatever it is, I'll paint it." I don't remember how long it took—I think it might have been just a few days—but I saw the painting in my head before I painted it, and I knew the name of it right then too.

All of those paintings that come to me like that are very significant because they seem to be the ones that people gravitate to more than anything else I've ever done. And then, of course, there are so many testimonies that go along with the known Christian images that I have done. I hear it so much that when people tell me how God blessed them, it's not anything uncommon; it's something that I expect to hear. One of the things I hear about "Forgiven" all the time is how many men and women would see the painting and right there in the store, fall to their knees crying.

SM: When you were fasting and praying for "Forgiven," was that a commissioned painting?

TB: That's the first time I had ever done a painting for Dayspring and Ron DiCianni. Ron wanted me to come on with them after he had done a couple of successful prints for Dayspring. He came to my house to tell me a story about him and God... apparently God let him know that I was somebody he was supposed to contact. I had never done anything like that before, but I said, "Let's see what happens." ...I tried to come up with some ideas but...every time I try to come up with something in my own flesh or that I think would be cool... it's boring! It just doesn't do anything.

That's why I have abandoned trying to create anything spiritual—when I do any kind of spiritual painting—I abandon any of that. All I do now is go to God, and then I wait on Him. And He gives it to me. So I won't even attempt anymore from this point to try to create something like that on my own, because once you've tasted what God can do, why in the world would I want to stick these little, crummy, fleshy hands into some kind of "know nothing" painting that might be pretty? It doesn't do anything. One thing about God: when He gives you a painting like that,

He puts an anointing on it. And another thing I've learned about the Lord is this: when God anoints a painting, it doesn't matter how good you are talent-wise, because when God anoints it, you could paint a stick figure, and it will still have the same power.

SM: I believe God is doing something in the arts, that He wants to free up Christian artists and to train them how to listen to Him, just like what you're talking about. There are a lot of Christian artists out there who are still coming up with their own ideas and still struggling to make something happen, and they find it hard to let go. You are describing to me that you let go of your preferences, what your preconceived notions are, and then you let Him use you. What would you say to the people who are having a problem making that jump? How could they go about that?

TB: First of all, they've got to trust in the Lord. They've got to trust in Him and His power and not in their own abilities. That's one of the things that can hinder somebody from being open to being really used. I'm not saying just because you come up with your own ideas that God won't anoint it or you don't have an anointing on your paintings, because I've seen it work both ways. Every painting that I do, I don't fast about. I do pray about them, but every painting I do, I don't fast on. They come different ways; I can tell you about the ones that have come through fasting and prayer, and I can also tell you about the ones that He's just thrown in my lap too.

SM: How do you pray about your art when you're working on it?

TB: Almost everything I do, when I'm working on a painting now, I pray to Him about. I just ask Him to help me get the image, bless me with it, help me get the right colors down. When I'm doing a color rough, I'll pray about that, because I really do need Him to help me break some of that stuff because some of that takes time. Not only that, I have to admit that I've noticed this too, a lot of times when I'm working on a painting, especially one of those that He gives me, it seems like in my life all hell breaks loose.

SM: I've experienced that before!

TB: So that happens quite a bit, so I'm always praying through it anyway because the truth of the matter is, I have no choice. It's usually a struggle to get through a lot of it.

A lot of artists, like you said in the beginning, still don't [operate on a deeply spiritual level in their work] or really understand it to the point of what we are talking about.

SM: Maybe a lot of them haven't had a taste of what God wants to do and what He can do.

TB: Well, I'm sure that's it. Because I've spoken to a lot of people, a lot of artists, about trying to figure out how to release or how to do that. How do I let go? How do I allow God to work through me? And it takes time, I mean everything that I've done, I learned…God taught me. It didn't happen overnight; it happened over a number of years.

Let me tell you how this all started for me. I was going through a three-year depression in the early 1980s, and I came out of it in 1983. This happened right afterward.

I never really wanted to do Christian artwork. All the great paintings had been done, and who am I to try to compete with the masters? I wasn't even interested in that. A friend of mine who was an actor, singer, and musician came to visit, and he told me a story that changed my life. He said there was a time when he felt God wanted him to do something with his life, and he wasn't sure what it was, so he went on a three-day, three-night fast to find out what God wanted him to do with his talent. He did not want to do Christian music, because he thought it was boring, the same thing I thought about Christian painting.

He said by the last night of the fast, he hadn't heard anything, so he was laying on his bed praying, and he said, "God, when are you going to tell me?" He listened and felt God said, "When you wake up tomorrow morning, I'll tell you." He jumped on the side of the bed in the morning and listened, and he felt God said to him, "I want you to do *My* music."

He said, "Oh, God, I don't want to do Christian music!" Then he heard God say, "I didn't say I wanted you to do Christian music; I want you to do My music."

When my friend said that to me, it was like a chill went up and down my spine, and I knew God was saying to me through his story, "I didn't say I wanted you to do Christian artwork; I want you to do *My* artwork." And that changed everything for me, because that made me realize I wasn't going to put God in a box anymore. God was letting me know, "Thomas, I'm going to do a new thing in you, something you've never seen before. Just trust Me." So from that point on, I said, "Whatever You want me to do, God, I'll do it." And that's how it started.

After that happened, it was like I was in school with the Lord, because He was teaching me stuff that I wasn't getting anywhere else. He said, "Watch what I'm going to do to your artwork." Here I was, an illustrator for 14 years, and He started showing me that He could take anything I did, and if He put an anointing on it, it was going to have an effect on people who saw it.

He taught me that there is a whole other life to a painting. I had heard that before but didn't know what it meant. I know what it means now. There truly is an aspect to artwork that is alive. God has done something in the creative process with art where once the art leaves your hands, it takes on a life all of its own that has nothing to do with me.

There is a spiritual thing that is going on while I'm working. I have this thing, and I'm sure a lot of artists do, that while I'm working on the painting, sometimes I become the painting. Say it's an animal or a certain type of individual or clouds or whatever; I have to think, *How can I paint the feeling of what that is?* It's almost like being an actor, but because I've been doing this so long now, it's kind of like second nature. And of course, He just does the rest.

After I painted "Forgiven," Dayspring wanted me to do a painting, and I was like, "God, how am I going to top 'Forgiven'?" I went through that struggle of trying to top myself with what God gave me, and He taught me something even in that. What He taught me was, "You paint what I give you to paint. Don't worry about what happens to that painting or what it does. I am the one who will see what will happen with that painting. I am the one who had you paint it for a purpose. No matter what I give you, don't worry about whether it's going to top this or that; just be obedient and do what I tell you to do, and I will do what needs to be done with the painting."

Did you hear about the 9/11 thing? I did a painting of the Statue of Liberty, and she's got a tear coming down her face, and Jesus is coming down in the clouds behind her...in all His glory. The thing that's so significant about that is that I got the idea two years before the incident happened, and I painted it five months before the incident happened. And when the painting came out, it finally hit most of the Christian bookstores the week of September 11. That's the first prophetic painting He gave me. For the last couple of years, I've had a few different people tell me that God was going to use me in a prophetic way. I didn't know what they meant until this thing with 9/11. It blew me away.

Here is a thought: everything that's fantastic, everything that's cool, that's magical and mystical and enchanting...all the beauty, all the Disney stuff, the wonderfulness of childhood, all that stuff that makes you excited about life—all that was created by God. Satan is the one who distorted it. All this cool stuff that has been distorted by satan, the originator of it is God. But because of satan's influence, everybody is afraid to have anything to do with that stuff. But I'm saying to God as an artist, as a creative person, "God, You are the originator, the Creator; there are things that we have never seen before, things that are cool, that will blow away what we think is so magical and cool now. Tap me into that stuff, so that we can produce things as artists that have the same effect as Star Wars, have the same effect as Harry Potter, but points to you."

Ron DiCianni

Ron DiCianni is a renowned Christian painter who gained notice with the cover illustrations of Frank Peretti's novels and has collaborated on over fifty books. He is a prolific artist whose vivid paintings are available in virtually every Christian bookstore in America. (See his work at Art2see.com.)

Like Thomas Blackshear, DiCianni makes a point to seek God throughout the projects he works on. He also believes in identifying the subjects God has given him a passion for and then doing his homework to understand them. He was at home in Chicago when I talked with him.

DiCianni told me that he sometimes has painters call him and ask how they'll know what to paint. In my interview with him, he said:

> I turn the question back on them and say, "When you're on your knees at night, what makes you cry?" It may be marriage or abortion or crime or evangelism. So that's [how it works] for me. And when I begin to sense those needs, and the Holy Spirit makes it obvious to me, they begin to germinate, and I can tell which ones last and which ones don't. Then God begins to direct me in His Word as to what those answers are and normally—I can't

say this always—normally I see the painting totally finished before it's ever done. The bad part of that is I could never do it as well as I've seen it. That's because God is implanting something in my mind to strive for, and humanly I'm able to come only as close as I'll allow God to do it through me.

Once I've visualized it, I begin to sketch and research. A lot of times my pastor becomes involved at that point, because I'm not a scholar; I'm not a theologian. I'm not very bright, to be honest, so put all those things together and you get a guy who doesn't know how to figure out a lot of stuff, and I'm not being falsely humble here, just really honest with you. Some things I think I'm pretty good at, but in other things, like studying, I've always had a very difficult time. So I'll go to my pastor…and say, "Could you help me figure this out and tell me that if I were doing a painting on this subject how would I picture this and what does this mean?" That has become a very, very wonderful aid. When I get people around me who are able to input from a godly standpoint, especially people like my pastor, man, it really helps the process along.

At that point I start sketching, composing, deciding if it's going be vertical, horizontal, etc. I'll usually bounce those sketches off of whoever I'm working with [publisher or my own company] and go, "Here's what I'm thinking," and sometimes they'll add to it. Then you come back and a lot of technical things begin to take over… There is never a time…in my studio, there is no such thing as, "OK, God, I can take it from here." [Up] to the moment that I'm giving it into the hands of [publishers or others]…most of the time it's with a prayer on my lips that says, "God, I know You wanted to do more, and I apologize. I only let You go that far, but I know You can take it and use it." And I've gotten some of my best stories from the ones I thought I failed the most on.

DAN HASELTINE

Haseltine is the lead singer of the multiplatinum and multiple Grammy-award-winning group Jars of Clay, one of a handful of Christian bands that have scored crossover hits on mainstream radio.

Haseltine feels his process of collaborating with the Holy Spirit is more mysterious, with the fruit often seen later. He tries to not have an agenda when he writes a song, leaving room for God to bring ideas. We sat down to talk before a Jars of Clay concert in Cincinnati. In a *Christianity Today* article, Dan had mentioned that he sometimes felt God "pushing the pen a bit." I asked him to talk about that.

Dan Haseltine (DH): I think when we sit down to write lyrics for a song…I go through this small crisis of "You know what? I have nothing to say." …So it really is a powerful move of the Spirit when we start the writing process…. What are the ideas, the concepts that we want to…communicate to the Church and the watching world? I really feel like the Holy Spirit comes in, and a lot of times the proof of that is simply that we'll finish a record, and the song will hit radio, and I still won't know what the song is really about until people start telling me. I hear stories from people saying, "This song meant this to me" or "It was about this," and it's overwhelming. You go, "Wow, this is really amazing, it's not at all what I started to write the song about. I put some lyrics down on paper; we sang them, and the Holy Spirit came in and…breathed life into them." When I say God is "pushing the pen," a lot of time it's because I don't know what I'm writing…. Sometimes weeks or years later, the song will have a very strong relevance to something in my life or something in the life of people that we're in contact with. It's powerful that way.

SM: How do you put yourself in a place where the Holy Spirit is able to move through you as a Christian artist?

DH: There have always been so many jokes about a broken heart being a songwriter's greatest asset…the bleeding-heart artist. I think it's very true…a contrite heart, and a humble heart. Opening yourself up, not having an agenda about what you write about. Simply just kind of laying yourself out there and saying, "Lord, I desire to be used, I desire to write songs for You, about You."

SM: Not having an agenda…that's so big. As an artist, you want to express yourself. How do you let go of that?

DH: I mean for me it really becomes a dialogue. It's a dialogue between me and God, to where it doesn't really matter how I'm presenting it necessarily, when I'm writing a song at first. When I start in that creative process, if I can truly keep it as having a conversation with one person, it's less about trying to communicate to the masses. I think we can put a lot of pressure on ourselves when we're writing to do it in a way that appeals to a broader audience, and that, I think, is the Holy Spirit's job. He is the one who makes Scripture come clear in people's minds and their hearts, and I think He does the same thing with truth in other forms. People will hear it and recognize it and take it in when the Holy Spirit draws them to that. I think you want to pull the pressure off yourself when you're writing, to not worry so much about it, I guess, and just sort of trust the Holy Spirit to do what He does and just be obedient and hopefully be in a place where you're asking God, "What does it look like for me to serve You in this place, with this gift?"

SM: Have there been times when, in prayer, you've received some creative direction or inspiration?

DH: Yeah, certainly. There have been times when lyrics have come to me just while in prayer. It's funny, because a lot of times lyrics come to me when I'm in church. Which means one of two things—either God is inspiring me through the sermon, or I'm not listening to the sermon [laughter]! I get a lot of creative energy from just being in an atmosphere of holiness, when I'm around people who are pursuing God…and it's easy to kind of lay my heart out on the table, which is really what I like to do in my lyrics; I like to put things out there that don't have easy answers, things that I struggle with. So when I'm in that sort of atmosphere that seems to be created by the Spirit, it's easier to kind of lay bare your heart and open up.

I think it's the songs that hit me that are the most personal, are the ones that I feel like the Holy Spirit is most present in, because on a general level, I'm not really a very open person about my emotions or just the kind of struggles that I have. It's not really what I like to do. People that know me know it takes a long time to get to know me. So when a song comes out that is just very transparent...like "Valley Song," ...it's a song about suffering and what it looks like to trust God in ...suffering. It was written around the time one of our band members [had a] sister-in-law who died suddenly of a blood clot. At the same time, we had some [married] friends, and the wife ended up dying of cancer. I think they were married six months. All these things like that were coming around.

We were really praying that God would give us a way to communicate some of that, and we sat down one afternoon and just started writing this song. It took all of about ten minutes to write the song, which is very quick for us. But it was one of these songs where you just felt this emotion pouring out, you felt the words just kind of flowing and keep coming, and it was just very obvious that that was the Spirit moving collectively in that room.... Everybody in the creative process just felt the weight of what we were writing about. That kind of thing, when you feel God just pouring these words out of you; you don't really know why. I just try to keep up, just keep writing. After we record it, I'm able to take a step back and listen to it and go, "OK...what does this mean?"

Peter Furler

Furler is the lead singer of the multigold-selling, phenomenally successful Christian band The Newsboys and co-founder of Inpop Records

Furler says he prays every day for new songs, believes that God is going to give him something—a lyric, an idea—and makes a point to listen to what the Spirit is saying to him. On a Newsboys tour bus in April 2000, before one of their shows in Indianapolis, I asked him how the Holy Spirit works with him in his creative process.

PF: Usually I recognize it later…. Sometimes maybe it's emotional, sometimes musically something happens. I think the best example would be this: For me…onstage the thing that I dread the most is sharing at the end of the night, not because of the message, just because it's uncomfortable for me; public speaking is not something I like to do. So there are nights when I walk offstage and I feel like I've bumbled everything…. I didn't make sense, and I contradicted myself. Those are the nights when the most happens… which I guess [shows] when we are weak, He is strong. And there are nights when I felt like I had all the points lined up and everything, and I don't get any reports back.

I pray for the Holy Spirit during the show, especially at the end of the night I want to welcome the Holy Spirit because I know that's where lives are changed. That's how people's hearts are broken, because of the Spirit. When it comes to writing a song, I'll usually feel it later, it'll be two albums later, and I'll hear a song on the radio and think, *Where did that come from?* …Even the message becomes newer to me…. It can be revealed to me right then and there what the Holy Spirit was saying.

I believe that God gives us talents, and we can bury them, or we can take them out and polish them and make them better for His glory. That's why when I sit down and write songs, I try to get better at it. But I do believe the power is in the Spirit…no matter how good I get as a song-writer, without the Spirit, it's going to be kind of dead, especially in what we do. There is power in words, but the Spirit has a different power that's not a word power, not a sight power; it's not a might power; it's not a strength power; it's just its own thing.

SM: Is there a way that you welcome God into your work?

PF: I believe songs come from revelation; they get revealed to you. I pray for songs, probably daily; I would say daily, to be honest. And when they come, I'm thankful, because I know where they come from. It is that process of going through and believing for something to happen. Not a matter of wanting a hit. Sometimes I think where the Holy Spirit becomes involved is where there is sort of a deep intercession where I can't even pray words…but I know God knows what I want. I've got this on my heart, and I want to put this into song.

SR: Have you felt a time when maybe He's given you a line or a word…?

PF: Oh, all the time! I believe they all come from Him. Whether it be by reading a book…it's like once again, the Holy Spirit reveals things to you. You can read Scriptures all your life, and know the Bible back to front, and until it's really revealed to you here [the heart], which I believe is the Holy Spirit…when it gets revealed to you, you know the God that I pray to is the same God that Moses prayed to.

God doesn't know time, He's not involved in time and space; we're involved. We start to die the day we are born, and things grow old to us quickly; the sun rising and setting grows old to us, but to God it doesn't, I don't think. He's probably still just as jazzed with the sun going around the earth…so when things get kind of revealed to you…[it] doesn't mean you're more holy—just at the right, appropriate time, the Holy Spirit reveals things to each and every one of us that is maybe what you need to hear at the time, or maybe it's what you need to know for what you have to prepare for coming up.

SM: Have you had some instances when God has given you a creative idea in prayer?

PF: Yeah, I've definitely had that. Usually the best thoughts come from the deepest of the deepest well…you can be writing a lyric, and you can write down, "I'm not ashamed of the gospel of Jesus Christ," and even though it's a very powerful thing, it can be very used and abused and come off as trite in that part of our minds that becomes jaded, that becomes fleshly, skeptical…. Then the Holy Spirit goes, "You know what, this is the truth…this is where I stand right now." …So that's where the Holy Spirit works wonders for me…. I'm sitting there and I write a lyric out and I go, "You know what? Two years ago I would have really thought that was a trite lyric, but I just feel that's what I have to say now." There is a revealing there. There is a confirmation. I think confirmation is the word; that's what the Holy Spirit does to me a lot of times in [writing] songs is confirming, "That's right; that's what needs to be said from you now."

You can be writing certain songs and just feel a revealing like, "You know what, I've heard that statement a thousand times, but now in this form it just really feels fresh." I think it's [that] the Holy Spirit breathes new life onto it. And you can't explain it; you can't go "Oh, this slogan's just become 'in' now...." No, this is truly fresh.

SM: And there could be a point where if you're not listening to the Holy Spirit you might miss out.

PF: Exactly! Without the Holy Spirit, you would definitely miss out on something. Because, once again, it gets back to God being younger than all of us, it seems. God knows no beginning and no end; we're the ones who grow old and die. The Holy Spirit keeps us youthful, keeps that flame burning, that flame of youth. I don't mean physical endurance; I'm talking about the flame that keeps us like little children. You can hear "Jesus is Lord" a million times, and you can hear "God loves you" a million times, but until the Holy Spirit takes that evidence and transfers it from apologetics to the human heart, it isn't anything. So that's what the Holy Spirit's for.

Buzz McLaughlin

Mclaughlin is a playwright, founder of The Playwright's Theatre of New Jersey, film producer, and the author of *The Playwright's Process.*

For McLaughlin, guidance from the Holy Spirit has come in the form of nudges, instant mini revelations, characters that are brought to life for him and write their own dialogue, and specific direction that has been spoken clearly into his mind.

McLaughlin and I first spoke about this at The New Harmony Project, a writers' conference in southwest Indiana. We followed up with a conversation on the phone, and he talked about listening to the Spirit in this way:

Buzz McLaughlin (BM): I always offer the writing up as kind of a holy act. There are many, many examples in my own writing days when I'm having a problem that I need to solve…. I'm always sending up little prayers and getting answers. Sometimes you have to listen very closely…sometimes it's a whisper you have to learn to listen to very keenly. I am offering it up, and I'm asking for guidance, and I'm opening myself up to be used by the Holy Spirit and for the Holy Spirit to really guide me, and sometimes all He needs to do is just plant a gentle nudge in my brain, just a tiny little breeze of an idea. I've learned to become extremely sensitive to that and go with those things, because I've learned how to kind of feel when that's happening.

It's really kind of mysterious how that occurs. It's called "the creative process"; see, a non-Christian would interpret everything I'm saying as "the creative process," but I'm very aware that a lot of these things are coming from outside myself. I've had instances where the characters would take over the scene in my mind. I'd just be transcribing what these people were saying, and I would be putting it down on the computer, and I would be absolutely amazed because I wasn't consciously thinking up what they were going to say. This is on a good day. I was just writing down what they were engaging in with each other—an argument, a conflict—and it would go on for pages like that. I would be very excited because I knew I was tapping into…you know, the Holy Spirit was kind of grabbing me in a Roman handshake. I was really fused with God here in the creative process because it was beyond my consciousness. And that happens on good days to me in all my plays.

And then, of course, you have days like bad prayer days, where it's just hard to feel like you can open up the ceiling and get into a good connection. But that's just our frailty as human beings operating there.

In the play *Sister Calling My Name*, even the title was a gift from God. I like to have a title when I'm writing a piece, because it tends to excite me and keep me going and [to] realize I have a work in progress that has potential. I remember the morning when the Holy Spirit handed me that title. I said a prayer about it, and I said, "I need some help on this; could You help me come up with a title?" Nothing happened, and I frittered around for an hour or so; then I took a walk around our pond in the woods and was thinking about it, and I came back, sat down, and about five minutes later the name just popped into my head, *Sister Calling My Name*. It's a perfect title for the play…it has a resonance to it, and you wonder kind of, "What's that all about?" Once you know the play, it's much better, because it's really what the play is all about; a sister calling back her estranged brother after 18 years and their reunion together. The minute it came into my head, I knew that was going to be the title for the play. It was this kind of magical moment you feel or elation and realizing that you were just handed something from outside of yourself. That's the feeling I get when that happens.

That play's been produced a number of places and won a number of awards and so on. What I find most interesting about that play, and my work with it once it's been produced, is that there have been people who have had conversion experiences because of the play, a number of people. And my strong sense is: that is what God was interested in when He helped me write that play. Actors especially are so moved that they start going back to church and feel like they have kind of reconnected with their spiritual lives. Even one producer of the play went back to church and became a regular churchgoer because of the play.

One story of God's guidance that Buzz tells actually occurred while he was working on a home project, but it has rippled out to affect his life and work. A while back, he and his wife bought some wooded property on a ridge in New Hampshire that he sort of envisioned as a sculpture; something he would clear and shape and form until it became his vision of a country retreat. He had decided to design a winding road that would get to the top of the hill, and there was a spot where he couldn't decide which way to go, whether to a flat area off to the left or up steeper to the right. He said:

> It was key, because it would affect the entire property in the future. I looked at it for two days... because I was going to bring in guys with big equipment to actually cut the road in with bulldozers and backhoes, and I just couldn't figure it out. I was always in a prayerful mood when I was up there, but finally I stopped...and said "God, what am I supposed to do here? These guys are

coming in three or four days. I have to figure out which way to go; this is a huge decision. What should I do?" And as soon as I said that prayer, it was like a voice outside of myself that said, "Buzz, always take the high road." It was God speaking to me! Almost like from Genesis or something. And the minute those words came into my head, I knew what to do—to put the road up the steep side—and that's where it is today. I was in the midst of a creative act, and I don't think of building this farm I built as much different creatively than writing a play. It a different kind of activity, but the creative process is very similar.

The interesting thing is that this word went beyond the actual work I was working on at the time; "Buzz, always take the high road," was something that went far beyond where I should put my little roadway up to my farm. It was telling how to live my life. How to become a better man in my life.

That is a mark of God's movement and leading in our creative process and our lives; God often accomplishes multiple things all at the same time—like giving Buzz one line that had a specific meaning for his immediate need but that also spoke to his entire life. At the same time, the giving of that word profoundly affirmed God's presence, love, and mercy to Buzz's listening heart. For most, Buzz included, this kind of clear word won't happen every day, but as you seek and listen, you may be surprised to find that it is possible.

GARY BAYER

Bayer is an actor and director based in L.A. and Jerusalem who has appeared in several movies and dozens of theater productions and television shows, including *Home Improvement*, *L.A. Law*, and *Knots Landing*.

Gary roomed with me while in Indianapolis to edit a film, and we had several enjoyable conversations about God and creativity, parts of which are incorporated here. I recorded his *Psycho 3* story while we were at The New Harmony Project. Bayer talks about his process:

> First I would seek Him about what I do, because I'm tired of running off on rabbit trails. And if He knows the plans He has for us, then He has designs. He says, "I've already got things that I've set up for you to do...with *Me*." I mean, he's allowed me to partner in things that He's doing! That blows me away. It's not like, "Run out there in the forefront and I'll come along beside you." No, He's saying, "These are things I'm about; I ask you to be a part of it." So it's His idea to begin with. Then, once that's clear—what I should do— the second thing I do is ask how I should do it.

Gary is a storyteller. Here is one wonderful story he told me a while back about how God worked through him in a most unusual way.

> I had auditioned for *Psycho 3*, and I thought, *Oh God, am I just so hungry that I'll take anything?* And yet I was willing to let go of it. But I had prayed

and lifted the script up [to God], physically, which is what I was doing at that point, actually lifting the scripts up to God as a reminder and a request for Him to lead. I was trying my best to allow God to close the door and was somewhat ambivalent, because I didn't know if I wanted to be seen in this kind of a thing. But they said, "It's gonna be more like the first one, not all bloody like the second one—more of a mental crusher."

They sent me up for this Catholic priest. They said it was a good role. I read the script and was just waiting for him to do something dorky; usually any man of the cloth in a film has some hidden perversion just waiting to come out. Well, it fascinated me in the script that…he went into the very bowels of climax and all of the stabbings and everything scared, but he remained true to being a man of God. He took a stand as a man of God, in the final climax of the killings. I thought that was really interesting; you don't see that.

So I auditioned for Mr. [Tony] Perkins, who was directing as well, and got the role! So we started shooting, and the very first day I remember getting on the set and I had, at that time, a little *Jesus Person Promise Book*, by David Wilkerson, that had been given to me by my brother when I first became a believer. It fit in my hip pocket really well. I had it there all the time, and I'd sweat through that thing. It fell apart I don't know how many times. I journaled in it, I wrote notes in it, I taped it back together; it looked like some little ancient manuscript. I'd read it on the subways in New York.

Anyhow, I was over in the corner thinking I'd have a little quiet time because they weren't to my scene yet, and I was all set to go. They'd put me through wardrobe and makeup and everything. So I was thinking I was all by myself in the corner reading, and I all of a sudden felt this presence like someone was staring at me. I looked up over my left shoulder and there above me was looming the frame of Tony Perkins. He was looking down on me saying, "Uh, what are you reading?" in his distinctive Anthony Perkins voice. I was not bold; I could feel sweat break from my temples, and I tried to, like, cover and close the book up.

And he said, "Some kind of manuscript? Old-lookin' thing! I love old-lookin' things!"

And I said, "Well, it's uh, uh…verses."

And he said, "Verses! Oh, I love verses! Like poetry?"

"Well, no, no…No."

"Well, what kind of verses?"

"Well, they're, they're…theistic."

He said, "Theistic! Oh, like pantheistic? I love Greek mythology…pantheistic verses?"

And sweat was popping out more, and I said, "N-n-no. More like, um, monotheistic."

He said, "Monotheistic?"

"Mmhm. Like, you know, New Testament, Old Testament...."

And he said, "Ahh. So, are you a...Christian?"

And I thought, *Oh gosh!* And said, "Yes."

He said, "Mmm. You have kids?"

"Yes, I do."

"And do you go to Sunday school with them?"

"Mmhm. I do."

"Ahh. So...you belong to a church?"

I thought, *Oh man, we're goin' nowhere fast. Very first day, and I haven't even gotten to scene one.*

He said, "Have you ever read Mahatma somebody?"

"No, I haven't."

"You never heard of him?"

"Uh, no."

"Well, I personally know him, and I have asked him questions. He's one of the foremost thinkers today. He makes you realize just how archaic religions really are. I must get you a copy. I would give you mine, but it's all marked up and underlined, and I hate reading other people's marks, so I'll get you a fresh copy."

So, off he went. Well, this started a couple of weeks of daily dialogue that was rather barby for the first two or three days and then settled into some kind of a serious inquiry into why I believed what I believed. Later, we got to shoot a scene where there is this woman who's been brutalized, and she's in the hospital, and I come to sit with her. Before I talked to her, I was sitting there reading a magazine or something, and Mr. Perkins yelled, "Props! He needs to be reading something! Ya got a *Playboy* back there?"

I said, "Mr. Perkins, would he really…?"

And he said, "Uh, yeah. You got a *Field and Stream*?"

I said, "Mr. Perkins, if he's a priest and he's there to encourage, what about that book of verses I was reading?"

"Oh, perfect! It's old-lookin'! Yeah, that'd be perfect!"

So I was sitting there in that scene reading my little *Jesus Person Promise Book*! Nobody knew except me and Mr. Perkins! Well, I happened to tell one of my pastors about this whole encounter that was going on, and he said, "Wow, you ought to give him your promise book!"

I said, "Are you out of your mind? That was one of the first things given to me as a believer. I have journaled notes, and it's falling apart anyway."

"Well, I thought you said he liked the look of it."

"Yeah, but it's my personal thing! And besides, he doesn't like things that are underlined, other people's things. He doesn't like that."

So I felt safe. So time went on, and we had these daily little exchanges about faith. He told me he liked science fiction, and I asked him if he'd be interested in reading C.S. Lewis' sci-fi trilogy. He said he would and promised to get me Mahatma somebody. I thought, *This is a good deal; we'll trade and I can hang on to my* Jesus Person Promise Book.

The last day of the shoot came, and I get to the trailer. I walked in, and lo and behold, there on my couch was a copy of Mahatma somebody. It was [Mr. Perkins'] personal copy—with his underlines and everything. So, I thought, *OK God, I'll give him my promise book.*

So, I finished my last scene, and I went back into the sound stage with my book in my hip pocket, where it always resided. I went over to Mr. Perkins, and he was just swarmed with crew and producers. Must have been 50 people around that guy. And I thought, *This is not the time to do this.* I thought it just wasn't meant to be, and I went back out in my trailer, and I got convicted. I thought, *OK God, I*

don't have another job today; I can sit here and wait.
I said, "If you want him to have this, bring him
out here." I thought, *That's pretty safe 'cause he's not
gonna come out here.* And in about 15 minutes, out
he came! But he was followed by this beehive of
people all around him. He made his way into the
makeup trailer, because he was also starring in [the
movie].

So I followed him into the trailer and had some
small talk, but it just didn't seem appropriate. So I
went back out and sat on my steps again. Finally,
everybody and Mr. Perkins came out, and they
headed back into the sound stage. About 20 feet
from the soundstage, all of a sudden, his entourage
took off ahead of him, and he was there by himself. And I shot up off my little stoop and headed
over to him. I got his attention, and he turned
around. He was always so nonfocused. I said, "I
want to thank you for giving me your personal
copy of [Mahatma somebody]. I know you hadn't
intended to do that. I would like for you to have
my personal copy of my *Jesus Person Promise
Book.*" And for the first time, all of this nonfocused stuff stopped, and he looked right at me.
All movement seemed to stop. He put his hand
out. I stuck my promise book in his hand. He
looked at me, put his hand around it, and said,
"Thank you. Thank you." He turned around,
stuck it in his hip pocket, and went off.

I stood there thinking, *Wow, he put it in his hip pocket just like I did.* I went back, gathered my stuff up, and started walking off the lot to the car. There was a little railing on a rise overlooking the sound-stage area. I remember praying, saying, "God what was that all about? Why did you want me to do that?"

And all of a sudden my heart just broke, and I leaned over this railing just weeping, and I didn't know why. I just was overwhelmed, weeping. Several weeks later, we went to the screening. What I had loved about the father was the fact that he would make a stand as a man of God, fearful though he may have been; he made a stand in the midst of melee. Well, that part was left on the edit room floor! Totally cut from the movie! That blew me away, and they also decided to go ahead and do graphic stuff. It was so graphic that my wife had to walk out. I thought, *I'm not telling anybody I did this.* I thought it was gonna be something handled well and a good role, and I was blown out of the water.

About six months passed, and it came out in the news that Mr. Perkins had AIDS. Within a year of that time, he died. And I, to this day, don't know what God did with that. But that gave me great pause. That was such a wakeup call in terms of the fact that God is not a respecter of persons. God may use me in the creative process with the gifts He's given me, but for a totally different reason than I may think. We can become so myopic…we may not understand at all and have to be drug there, but that is a work of the Holy Spirit.

Gary asked for God to guide him in choosing that part and asked to partner with the Holy Spirit in using his talent. The project turned out to be what looked like a career mis-step—but in the middle of it, God used Gary to witness to a man who was nearly impossible to reach and on the brink of losing his life.

That is successful *collaboration with God.*

As these artists have discussed, you often don't see the immediate fruit of partnering with the Holy Spirit in the creative process. But, of course, that is no different than the life of faith or how the natural world works.

Walter Wangerin Jr. puts it this way: "Sometimes we're just ignorant and unaware, and for me, I'll go back to a book that I wrote years ago. I'll read that and I'll say, 'Who wrote this?' I remember sitting there, I remember working on this, and…it was brain labor. But I go back and read it and I say, 'Wow, there are thoughts in here I never knew before.' …I just look at the consequence and say, 'Well, *that* must have been divine.'"

Whether we feel God's presence in our process or not, we can be sure that He is there working with us if we let Him guide us in finding divine inspiration.

We definitely have a part to do
in finding divine inspiration.
We apply ourselves, develop our skills,
grow in our craft.
We turn our wills toward Him, discipline ourselves
to practice a listening lifestyle and
obey what He speaks to us.
We stand against the attacks of the enemy
and move forward in faith.
And God meets us as we move toward Him.
He provides the direction on what
to do and how to do it.
He inspires us with Holy Spirit
light and revelation.
He opens the doors of opportunity and brings us to
the right places in the right timing.
And He brings the anointing on the message that
gives the work the impact He wants.

CHAPTER 10

A FUTURE FOR THE ARTS

*No matter how good an artist you are—
I don't care if you're the greatest artist
who ever lived—you will never know how
good you could have been if you don't turn
your work over to the Lord.*

—Thomas Blackshear

THE FUTURE IS BRIGHT FOR CHRISTIAN ARTISTS. We can look forward to exciting times as we pursue finding divine inspiration and invite God to move in our creative process. How exciting to realize that we are part of a generation that is standing at the threshold of a New Renaissance!

This book has focused on the foundation that needs to be laid for artists to reach that goal of a renewal in the arts: growing our intimate, personal relationships with God and learning to hear His voice. Of course, there are other things that need to be developed for Christian artists to reach our potential, such as training in our field, skill development, and a desire for excellence. But one other key that is essential for the future impact of Christians in the arts is often overlooked. It is the necessity of immersion in Christian community.

It's so important for Christian artists, just like all other Christians, to find our place in Christian community. Sometimes we get off on our own or may have to spend a lot of time in isolation in order to do our work. That's understandable, but when we resurface from that place, God wants to draw us into Christian community.

The fact is, until we Christian artists really step into our God-designed place in the Body of Christ, something will be lacking in the Church. That may mean that we have to overlook biases against the arts, put up with ignorance about the arts, and suffer through aesthetic disasters in church for a while, but it's part of stepping up and becoming who we were made to be. And that will bring the Church closer to what it is meant to be; the shining Bride of Christ.

Progress has been made in this area in the last couple of decades; most sizable churches now play more contemporary worship songs. But even in that area, more can be done to develop singers and songwriters within congregations. There is something very powerful about singing a well-crafted, Spirit-inspired song written by someone in your own congregation. It brings a unity, an appreciation for God's gifts and the talents that He's placed in the community, as well as an electric sense of immediacy and relevance. All the other arts carry similar benefits as well. Imagine if they were allowed to be present in churches like worship music is; our communities might be overwhelmed with blessings from God!

COMMUNITY REACHING OUT TO ARTISTS

Of course, it's hard for churches to embrace the arts unless pastors and church leaders reach out to artists. Part of a leader's job is to reach out to people, but artists can sometimes take a little more initiative. We can be sensitive, shy, or cynical; guarded because of past experiences; or the opposite—dramatic, opinionated, or off the wall. We might seem a little strange or unconventional. But it's important for leaders to understand that learning to address and appreciate the artist's soul is good for everyone. The focused attention benefits the artist, because he is built to be part of something bigger than himself, to collaborate with community, and to receive and translate messages between God and His people. The leaders benefit by being stretched and seeing and embracing the intuitive side of God's personality through His artists.

It's so refreshing to realize that though study, sermons, and devotions do unmistakably facilitate growth in our faith, sometimes God just wants to speak to us in a profoundly intuitive way, through beauty and art. That realization can be like a deep, luxurious, cleansing breath for a community, and it reveals yet another facet of God's wonderful love.

There are many other benefits to reaching out to and discipling artists in the Church, some of which we touched on earlier. Their art and craftsmanship can bring growth, blessing, insight, and healing. Look at the way sculpture was used as a conduit for healing people physically, spiritually, and emotionally in the Bible, such as in the story of the bronze serpent in Numbers 21. Because of their grumbling and disobedience, the Israelites were experiencing a terrifying plague of venomous snakes that bit many of them. God instructed Moses to make a bronze snake and put it on a pole so that everyone who looked on it would be healed. This got the Israelites' eyes off of the situation—the snakes swarming around them—and gave them a specific point in time when they repented and were healed. The sculpture even blessed them with an image they could recall that healing with. It was an intuitive symbol, and each person could have his own personal experience with repentance and healing. Plus, not only did this symbol serve a desperate and immediate need, but it also spoke prophetically about Jesus' coming sacrifice on the cross and reminds future generations that God has loved and planned to rescue us for eons. Only a piece of artwork in the hands of the Holy Spirit can do all that. How can the Church not give such a powerful tool a regular place in community?

ARTISTS JOINING CHRISTIAN COMMUNITY

Steve Turner says in *Imagine*:

When I first came to London I attended a good church, but then began to think that the sermons weren't really addressing the issues that preoccupied me. To do that, I read books of theology. Pretty soon the reading of theology had replaced the church, and I was becoming what some people would call a Lone Ranger Christian.

I was making myself a special case. The majority of Christians needed the structure of the church, but as an artist, I didn't. I had nothing in common with ordinary churchgoers; they weren't my kind of people. The standards of presentation I expected were so much higher than the church's. Things presented as art—sketches and songs, for example—offended me because they weren't professional.

I wasn't alone. I knew many musicians, painters, poets, dancers and actors who felt uncomfortable in church. I had friends who thought that having a meal with a couple of Christians constituted fellowship and others who worshiped in the church of their own hearts. In many cases churches had failed to inspire and nurture these people. In other cases I'm sure that they had developed a false sense of self-importance and were being kept back by pride.[1]

Turner goes on to quote poet Jack Clemo from a BBC television documentary:

At first I steered clear of the church, having a sort of "poetry religion," but a Christian can't develop much on "poetry religion." We all need the religion of ordinary people and the love of other converts. That's why, in the end, I went back to church; to worship around people who don't like poetry. It's a good discipline. I can't put myself apart from them as someone very special. As a convert I am just an ordinary believer, worshipping the same Lord as they do.[2]

Actor Gary Bayer talks about this as well:

I like the sense of family, of being with people who don't necessarily do what I do. For one thing, the reason I think that's important for an artist is we're "tellers," and if we're not living out there and listening and watching and soaking up the very stuff of people and dynamics and life and sweat and rhythms that come into the stories that we tell, how can we really taste and know that and recreate that? We [artists] have a tendency to get real insular and then start to actually try to recreate what we see in the entertainment which is already fantasy or recreation, so we are several degrees removed from the source. We start copying what's already fabricated instead of living among the real.[3]

Dan Haseltine says about community:

I don't think artists can do what they do, in terms of being evangelical or having an impact on their culture at large, if they don't have a connection to the Church. When that relationship between the Church and the artist is severed or something happens there, a lot of times you'll really see the impact that they're able to have out in the community really suffer. I speak a little bit from experience, even with Jars of Clay. I know that when we were out playing in bars and clubs and places like that, we caught a lot of negative attention from the Church; they didn't really like what we were doing, and they didn't understand it. So rather than continuing to pursue the church, helping them understand what we do, we would get very bitter and kind of sever that tie. And we recognized that you're cutting yourself off from the root, so you're not getting fed, and you're basically just existing out there on your own strength.

Of course, God can certainly still work when you are disenfranchised from the Church, but I really feel that there is a direct lifeline the Church provides. The church community keeps you, as an artist, grounded foundationally and supported and keeps you learning. I think being connected to a body of believers and a pastor… is very important. That's one of the main things that's going to keep the Church completely relevant.[4]

Madeleine L Engle says, "The writer at the desk is indeed writing in isolation, but (for me, at least) this isolation must be surrounded by community, be it the community of family, village, church, city."[5] Authors Richard Foster and John Eldridge have both said that their books are written with the support of community.

Getting involved in the Christian community is one of the key factors to our success as listening Christian artists.

I've found this to be true countless times as I've prepared for and worked through projects and as I've sought to grow as a person and a Christian. A well-functioning church community is full of rich relationships, insight, and ministry opportunities that will affect your art profoundly. God designed the Christian community as a place where every Christian's gifting, large or small, can be discovered, nurtured, and used for the benefit of the Body of Christ. Romans 12:4-6 says, "Just as each of us has one body with many members, and these members do not all have the same function, so in Christ we who are many form one body, and each member belongs to all the others. We have different gifts, according to the grace given us...." There's great fulfillment in this discovery, and in using your gifts in church community—fulfillment artists sometimes miss.

Maybe you've already faced so much rejection and misunderstanding that trying to open up to church people who have little or no appreciation for art seems masochistic. Or maybe you've bought into the romantic idea that an artist must be an independent person, a rebel who makes art and doesn't need other people's approval. It's my belief that we need to find ways to overcome these barriers if we are to be effective Christian artists or "artists who are Christians." We have much to give to and much to learn from our brothers and sisters.

They need us to bring our unique insights to bear on the mystery and sovereignty of God, to balance dry, logical thinking with intuitive revelation. They need us to help them to see things (like creation, grace, or the human condition) in a new way. And we need them to speak into our lives and keep us accountable and to support us in prayer as we struggle to hear God's guidance in our work. Our brothers and sisters can help us know love that's not connected to performance or beauty or common interests but based on the bond we share as beloved children of the Father. The type of community involvement that I'm talking about rarely comes from just going to church on Sundays. It is fostered in personal contact, in getting together to eat, in praying together, and in ministering together.

THE ARTIST IN A SMALL GROUP

I am a big fan of small groups or home groups. You may have a bias against them, but hear me out. A good home group where there is sharing, interaction, and prayer (not just teaching—that would be a Bible study) is a wonderful place to share your gifts and insights and to pray and be prayed for—to really "do life" with other Christians.

So many times I've found at home group the support I needed just to get through another week of working in a totally worldly creative environment. I've found, if I will open up and share what I'm struggling with, that there is always a positive response. Once, when I shared with my home group the struggles I was encountering in writing this book—namely, spiritual, emotional, and mental attacks from the enemy—they responded with a sort of spiritual group hug. We prayed a lot about every area of this process of writing, and I left rejuvenated and encouraged, feeling loved and full of purpose. Recently, in looking back on my journal entry about that night, I noticed someone had said he felt God might be saying "the attacks would bring healing." After nearly a year, I realized that was happening. The points where I was vulnerable for attack were points where—as I prayed—God was healing and repairing. Rereading the journal entry was a wonderful confirmation, but that wasn't all. I made a point to let the person who spoke that word about healing know what an effect it had on me, which encouraged him and confirmed that he had indeed heard God's voice whispering. That's how community works— multiple people exercising their gifts for mutual growth and encouragement. If you don't have this in your church, con- sider praying that God either would bring community con- nections for you or guide you to another church.

For years the Indianapolis Vineyard had a small group that focused on developing artists. When we got together, we would spend time doing typical home group things— prayer, study, sharing what's going on in our lives—but we would also talk about new things we saw as artists that excited or interested us. This might include anything—a picture, a poem, a movie, anything inspiring. The study time also was geared for the artistic imagination. Then, on a regular basis, we would pick a night just to get together and create. We'd pray before we started and ask God for inspira- tion and ideas, and then let loose and do whatever we felt led to—writing, drawing, painting, music, and more. Occa- sionally we were asked to do a project for the church. One time we made a stunning mosaic; another time some paint- ings; another time we put together an entire service. This kind of group was a great place to grow gifts and skills, inspire one another, and plant a vision. (Look for *Finding Divine Inspiration* small group material soon.)

Another great function of community is to provide prayer support for the artist. Satan will attack those who push into territory that he has staked out, so Christian artists need to be ready for a battle. Practicing finding divine inspiration in the context of a listening lifestyle goes a long way toward winning those battles, but enlisting the prayer support of other faithful, mature Christians is so important.

I don't like to "bother" people with my needs, so my tendency is to try to do things alone, without any outside help. Plus, I'm not Billy Graham or some exciting nonprofit ministry, so it feels weird to send out e-mails asking for prayer on the projects God has given me, like this book. I don't want to appear self-important. But God has brought me to the end of my strength many times and forced me to push past my comfort zone and ask for prayer support. In fact, I developed a list of people I e-mailed with updates on this book. Their faithfulness, prayer, and encouragement are essential to creating a safe space where I can function as an artist in the pursuit of God. I could not have completed this book without their prayer support. They were a very real part of the collaboration that made it a reality.

God has given us all to one another in a unique and mysteriously wonderful way, and we must be obedient and press into Christian community to fully realize who we are individually and what we can be together.

THE VISION

The possibilities are magnificent for artists who embrace the things we've talked about for the last several chapters: artists whose lives and work are built on the foundation of a vibrant relationship with God, whose surrendered hearts practice daily collaboration with Him, and whose connection to Christian community is solid and fruitful.

Earlier in the book we talked about things that might be accomplished if a New Renaissance were to blossom—paintings, sculptures, photographs, music, inventions, design, architecture, and more that would reveal God's glory and draw people to Him would be plentiful. A whole new presence of God's Kingdom in the world could become unavoidably evident.

God has planned specific projects and ideas for all of us who long for this New Renaissance, and He'll reveal them to us as we seek Him. They may be simple and small or huge and breathtaking, and collaborating with Him to carry them out will change our lives and alter the world around us.

As I prayed about this section of the chapter, I felt God leading me to write less about specific ideas and more about attitudes and concepts. I asked Him to give me some thoughts and here's what ended up in my journal:

> The vision for the future of the arts starts with a whole wave of artists who would learn how to lay down pride and operate as clear, unselfish voices collaborating with the Holy Spirit to bring God's truth to the world.

> This wave of surrendered, God-collaborating artists would have an open door to educate churches and the Body of Christ on the divinely appointed purpose and potential of the arts.

> Congregations and fellowships would learn first-hand how God can speak directly to them through

Holy-Spirit-inspired art when artists demonstrate it with music, painting, sculpture, poetry, and more that brings prophetic messages to specific congregations.

Pastors and leaders would catch the vision of the unique place of the arts in spiritual growth. They would be so hungry to hear what God would say to their congregations through the arts that they would disciple and empower artists to operate as prophets and teachers.

It would become standard for the Church to train, equip, and support artists to operate as missionaries in the culture and the world. These empowered artists would be so full of the life of God that it would saturate their projects, not necessarily as a direct message but as feeling, a spirit, an overflowing of God's love through and in their work.

In the vision for the future, light would emanate from the Church through the arts in a unique and relevant way. Artists working in collaboration with God would invigorate the Church so much that it would become the patron and conduit of all things beautiful to the world, more than it ever has been.

Ask God to give you and your community of believers a vision for the arts where you live. Pray for your pastor and leaders to have a craving to see what God wants to say through the arts. Pray for open doors. Pray for a New Renaissance.

Is there something God has been
speaking to you to do
for a while—maybe years?
Maybe fear, procrastination, lack of skill,
or lack of confidence has kept you from it.
Take some retreat time now, a few hours
or a few days, and put it before God.
Ask Him to speak to you about yourself,
about timing, about steps you can take.
But before you look for answers to those questions,
make sure to take time to just enjoy Him
in prayer, in song, in the Word,
or in His creation.

Because no matter what you do or
haven't yet done,
He enjoys you.

CHAPTER 11

Q & A About Collaborating With God in Your Creative Process

Art is love. —Holman Hunt

INVITING GOD INTO YOUR CREATIVE PROCESS is easy. Just that simple act can change your art and your life. But learning to hear God's voice and develop a truly collaborative relationship with Him can take time. If you are like me, you'll have many questions along the way. This chapter takes a shot at answering a few of the common questions about the journey of developing a listening lifestyle. You'll also find more thoughts on the *Finding Divine Inspiration. com* Website.

WHAT IF I CAN'T SEEM TO HEAR ANYTHING OR I SEEM TO HAVE A BLOCK WHEN I'M TRYING TO HEAR GOD'S VOICE?

We talked in Chapter 6 about minimizing the voices that compete against the voice of God in prayer time. Identifying and dealing with them will go a long way to quieting your mind so that you can hear God's still, small voice. Sometimes the mind wanders because it's not used to quiet or a lack of stimulation. In this case, it helps to focus on an image of Jesus or the Father in your mind.

For me, that image has changed over the years as my way of relating to God has changed. When I was going through my life crisis, I was devastated, desperate, and humbled. The image I saw when I prayed was of God's feet and me clinging to them. Eventually, I started imagining more of His person, sometimes seeing myself curled up in Jesus' lap. Then, as I described in an earlier chapter, I began visualizing the Father holding my face in an intimate way, closely, as I had seen in a painting at church. I wrote that I was initially repulsed by the intimacy of that image but that God used it to break through the way I related to Him. It's been a great blessing ever since and continually provides needed focus in my prayer time.

Ask God to give you a picture that you can focus on in your prayer time. It may take a while, but He will bring it to you. He loves to use our imagination to bring us closer to Him.

It was mentioned in earlier chapters, but I should say again that there are times when we just won't hear from God very well, if at all. In that case, we just keep meeting with Him, pursuing our relationship with Him, and persevere through it. He may be working on our faith. When we take the time to invite Him into our creative process, He won't always overwhelm us with a sense of His presence. Often, hearing Him will require us to finely tune our ear to Him.

Whether we've become clogged with other voices or we haven't taken care of unforgiveness, we may feel like God is distant.

I have found that when I've checked all these things and still am not hearing, there may not be a reason that I can account for. If it is important that I get a project done, I move forward in faith, believing that guidance will come to me as I move and work. It just seems like there are some days, maybe even weeks, that I don't hear much guidance, just as AM radio stations come in more clearly some days than others. Sometimes you can wait for the inspiration to come. When you have the time to wait, take it and enjoy it.

If a blocked condition persists for a long time and you've addressed the hindrances we mentioned in Chapter 6, there may be a need to deal with a condition like the one Leanne Payne brings up in *Listening Prayer*. She says that she had a very emotional and exciting experience with God as a young child, "as if a living presence entered into her as a holy fire," causing her fingers and toes to tingle with joy. She "lived long in the glow" of that experience but became confused by the lack of ongoing feelings, finally falsely thinking that, since she could not feel or hear God, she must be estranged from Him.

There was a painting in Payne's childhood church of Christ as "The Light of the World" by Holman Hunt that had spoken to her as a young girl. But even after her conversion, she felt that Christ still was knocking on the door of her heart (as in the painting), but she just couldn't hear Him. She says:

Because I did not *feel* Him, I called to Him as if He were only and always far off. *He was there*, however, all the while as I was calling to Him. The problem was that I was estranged from my own heart; I did not know it and was therefore in effect absent from it and him. Being absent from my soul and not understanding it is a very modern kind of problem. I was walking 'alongside myself.' Like any materialist, I was trying and expecting to apprehend all of reality with my sensory being.[1]

Payne says that, if she were to speak to that little girl now, she would do this:

A little practical step is next, a way of praying that can help the Christian who would enter into listening prayer. This prayer helps the person see and hear with the heart. In this case I could pray in a number of ways. But because the Lord so used Holman Hunt's painting in her life, I would likely ask her, with eyes closed, to look up to Jesus with the eyes of her heart and thank Him for that painting. Then, depending on the Holy Spirit's leading, I might ask her to see in memory that painting, with Christ knocking on the door of her heart. I would then speak the truth to her about what was happening: "He is knocking because somehow you've forgotten He is with you. You've forgotten how to talk to Him and hear Him speak to you." Still depending, of course, on the Holy Spirit's leading—and it is perfectly amazing how wonderfully the Holy Spirit leads in these cases—I would ask her to see herself in her own heart and then, once she pictured this, to walk over and open the door and bid Jesus come in and talk with her.... After asking her what she was seeing, I would then ask her to listen to what He would say to her. I would ask, "What is the Lord saying to you, what is He speaking?" And she would hear and tell me, "Through a prayer that allowed me to see and hear with my heart—a prayer that allowed the intuitive-imaginative faculty to be exercised—the door would have opened quickly."[2]

As we've talked about, there are plenty of times when we just won't seem to hear God's voice, and we'll be required to move forward in faith. Dallas Willard thinks this is a part of becoming spiritually mature, that as we get to know Him better, we will develop the "mind of Christ":

So our union with God...consists chiefly in a conversational relationship with God while we are each consistently and deeply engaged as His friend and co-laborer in the affairs of the kingdom of the heavens.

I want to emphasize that there is an important place for blind faith in God's presence, as we have described it, as well as for the feeling or sense that He is near and for a display of the supernatural effects of His presence. But no amount of these can take the place of intelligible communication through word and shared activity.

When all of these types of presence are in place, it is then that the royal priesthood of the believer (Exodus 19:6) is realized as it should be. It is then that having a personal relationship with God becomes a concrete and common-sense reality rather than a nervous whistling in the spiritual dark.[3]

Now, here are a few questions about listening to God in the creative process.

What does it mean when I've sought God and listened during a project, but it "fails"?

Even though the act of creating a work was initiated and set up by God, the work itself may not be the point. There may be times when the *process* and what we learn through it may be what God wanted us to do and get. The finished work may or may not be an excellent work of art, but that doesn't mean the Holy Spirit was any less present. It just means that God's ways aren't our ways, and when we are yielded to Him and listening, He may take us down mysterious paths that at the time don't seem to further our career or position us properly. These can and do serve as challenges to examine where our focus and treasure is. Is our treasure and identity really in God, or is it in our gifts and abilities? We can *expect* these questions to be brought to us from time to time, and it may come in the form of a project that seems to fail.

I also find it incredibly gracious that God uses and seemingly even ordains our mistakes. This book is about striving for excellence in our creativity and going to new heights in our art by working in harmony with the Holy Spirit. But the other side of that is that we still are human and will often mess things up, and God is still God and will often allow things to happen that confound us. Sometimes it may be God's plan for us to make a mistake.

I am occasionally asked to do readings at our church, and it's an honor to use my voiceover skills in that way. I always pray for the Holy Spirit to speak through me, and I often feel His presence while I'm reading. On one occasion, the first service reading went flawlessly, but at the second service I bobbled a few words. It wasn't a big deal but left me wondering, *Did I not try hard enough? Should I have practiced more? Was God using this to speak to someone in the audience? Or was He trying to humble me?* (The answer to that one is almost always yes!)

I was thinking about this a little later as I connected with God one morning and felt I should flip open my *Purpose Driven Life* devotional book. The section I turned to was about Noah, which seemed appropriate, since he had been a man of great obedience but still messed up when he got drunk in his tent and lost all his clothes. I felt God was whispering to me as I read the encouraging Scriptures. Then He took out the bullhorn. Right there in the middle of the page of the devotional companion book for one of the best-selling Christian books of all time was a *mistake*. A word was clearly missing from one of the verses. I thought about the hard-working writer and editors who had missed that word, only to discover it after a gazillion books were printed. They probably thought, *Why did that happen? What's the point?*

At least part of the answer is that God used it to speak directly to me in a unique and beautifully gracious way. He let me know that I was heard, that He cared. And He strengthened my faith and once again brought home the principle, "...All things work together for good to them that love God, to them who are the called according to His purpose" (Rom. 8:28). *Especially* mess ups!

Here's one more interesting thing about failures and mistakes: occasionally, prior to something unusual that's happened with a creative project—particularly live projects such as that reading—God has gently warned me while I was praying beforehand. That was the case before that bobbled reading—I had felt Him saying this might not go as I expected. That softened the blow and allowed me to be at peace, and it caused me to look past the moment to see what He might be doing in the larger scheme of things. I've found these kinds of experiences to be a very cool benefit of living a listening lifestyle.

WHAT'S GOING ON WHEN I INVITE GOD IN, THEN DO "BAD" WORK?

You may need more training or development of your skills. There are times when God will miraculously compensate for our lack of skill and get His message across anyway; I have prayed to be able to paint beyond my ability and had that happen. But other times He may just be calling us to do our part in sharpening what He has given us. I've found it interesting that some of the initial tries that I took at new media, such as filmmaking, were met with some success, but subsequent projects in those fields required more discipline and knowledge. For some reason, God may be gracious to the beginner and then require more development later.

Don't be so sure, though, that God still won't use your "bad" work; if you've invited Him in to partner with you, He can use anything.

Another reason we may feel like we have done bad work that could not possibly have been inspired by the Holy Spirit is that we suffer from perfectionism; nothing is ever good enough for us. There is certainly much to be said for working on a project until you've done everything you can do and are able to walk away saying, "I did the best I could with the resources available to me at the time." That, coupled with a sense of spiritual release, is the way that I always hope to finish off a project. Perfectionism keeps on going, however, past the point of being done, obsessing that the work could be better. Many of us visit that place from time to time, but no one should live there. Michelangelo is reported to have struggled with this, resulting in many uncompleted sculptures in his later years.

When you are faced with the tension between trying to achieve excellence or crossing over into obsession, yield to the Holy Spirit and listen for His direction. He can provide the gracious sense of confirming when you are done. Depending on Him for this confirmation is a practical way to cast one more care upon Him in our creative process.

WHAT'S UP WITH PEOPLE WHO SAY THEIR WORK IS INSPIRED BY GOD, BUT IT JUST DOESN'T LOOK LIKE IT?

Once again, often that's very hard to know for sure and dangerous to judge. One way to avoid being someone who gives God the credit for things that don't seem to add up is to use the correct language. We try to hear from God, but we're not like the prophets of the Old Testament, like an oracle. So avoid definitive declarations like "God told me" or "This is the prophetic word of God" and use language like "I feel like God said" or "The Spirit seemed to be saying" or "I think this is what God was saying." I've tried to use that rule in this book.

God loves the expressions of His children, whether they are fit to be displayed or not. If a person truly feels that even though she has little talent, the Father has given her a desire to partner with Him in an artistic expression, then that is to be blessed. That doesn't mean the result will be displayed in a museum. When we assume that every creative impulse we feel is to be shared with other humans or the expression is tied to boosting low self-esteem, then there is error.

One of the reasons many Christian artists are hesitant to say that their work is divinely inspired is that they don't always feel it is "good." The thought is this: how could the Holy Spirit be a part of creating something that is less than excellent? Well, of course, there are two of us in this equation (more if you are collaborating with others)—One who *is* holiness, light, and perfection and one who is "becoming"— becoming more than a child, but still a child; made righteous and becoming holy, but *still* a struggling sinner. James said, "We all stumble in many ways ..." (James 3:2). Paul said, "For what I want to do I do not do..." (Rom. 7:15). We won't always get it right, but with time and experience in listening to the Holy Spirit, you'll build a string of successes in collaborating with God and the work He's given you to do.

I DON'T WANT TO DO ANYTHING UNLESS I HEAR FROM GOD. HOW CAN I BE SURE THAT I AM HEARING FROM HIM?

I can't tell you how often and in exactly what way you'll hear from God, or even if you'll recognize it. I can tell you that if you point every creative act toward Him, you'll know the fulfillment of collaborating with the Creator.

As we've talked about, it's very important to ask God to guide us to the projects He would have us get involved with. We certainly do not want to spend a lot of time on a project the Father hasn't intended for us to work on. Once you've built "a house" under the assumption that God wants you to, only to find out later that you dreamed up the idea on your own, you know the meaning of laboring in vain (Ps. 127:1). And you don't want do it again.

There can and should be, though, a place of freedom where we can just create—let it flow. Having asked God to be in our process, we might do whatever comes, without judging it. Then we are at liberty to sort it all out later, with the benefit of time and perspective, looking for the mark of the Holy Spirit. It's the same principle that I brought up in the chapter on developing a listening lifestyle; you write down what you think God might be speaking to you and then come back later to look at it. Sometimes letting things flow—in your journal and in your work—can be a good way to learn to discern His voice. Write or work as you feel

He's leading you to for a while; then come back later and see if you can discern the mark of the Holy Spirit. Do this consistently, and you may find it's easier to know when He was speaking to you or guiding you.

It's also important to not become paralyzed because we just don't know what God wants us to do. Sometimes we invite God into the process, and if we just don't discern any guidance from Him after a while, we still move forward in faith.

I was reading the classic book *Boundaries* some time ago and came across what the authors call the Law of Activity, which talks about how passivity can become the ally of evil.

> God expresses His opinion toward passivity in Hebrews 10:38-39, "But my righteous one will live by faith. And if he shrinks back, I will not be pleased with Him. But we are not of those who shrink back and are destroyed, but of those who believe and are saved." Passive "shrinking back" is intolerable to God; and when we understand how destructive it is to the soul, we can see why God does not tolerate it. God wants to "preserve our souls."
>
> ...This is also the way God has made us. If He "hatches" us, does our work for us, invades our boundaries, we will die. We must not shrink back passively. Our boundaries can only be created by our being active and aggressive, by our knocking, seeking and asking. (Matt. 7:7-8)"[4]

The *Boundaries* authors are not talking about pushing forward without prayer or negating the discipline of being still and waiting on God. They are talking about not walking in the light you have been given, not moving forward in what God is leading you to do, not stepping out in real faith and staying stuck instead.

God honors our desire to hear Him and receive His guidance in our lives and projects. He is thrilled when we defer to Him instead of following our own whims. But He wants to collaborate with us, and that means that our wills and our effort are involved in the process. By exerting our wills and effort, even in prayer and quiet waiting, we become people who believe and are saved, not people who shrink back. I'll say it again: the Christian life is a life of *faith*. Even if we could discern every whisper God speaks to us, we still would have to live by faith, stepping forward when we just don't know what is going to happen.

This is the path to finding divine inspiration:

we invite God into the creative process.

He changes us as we learn to hear His voice and desires.

The Kingdom of Heaven is brought into the world as we collaborate together.

CHAPTER 12

PRAYERS FOR CREATIVITY

THE EVANGELICAL PROTESTANT TRADITIONS THAT I WAS RAISED IN
have often shied away from written prayers, instead
preferring a more personal expression. Of course,
personal, specific, spontaneous prayer and petition is highly
important to our daily relationship with God, but I've also
come to observe that prayers developed and spoken by others and passed down over time can have a certain weight to
them. They can be helpful in setting a model for effective
prayer as well as conveying a sense of community with other
believers who have offered up similar expressions.

In the process of writing this book, I began looking for
prayers that artists had prayed through the ages. My search
for petitions that addressed creativity was mostly fruitless for
a long time, so I decided to ask God to lead me in con-
structing one using the insights in this book. That thought
was on my mind very late one Saturday night as I whispered
a prayer and turned off the light. Within moments, words for
a creativity prayer came rushing into my semi-consciousness.

I turned the light on and wrote the phrases in my journal, not worrying if they made sense. The light went on and off a few more times that night, as I felt compelled to scribble the words that came. Here's what it looked like in the morning, with only a few edits.

THE CREATIVITY PRAYER

Lord my God, as I prepare to work using the talents You have given, please free me of my self-imposed limitations. Pull down the walls and boundaries I have set up or that have been set up for me through family, experience, or fear.

Purify me and let me hear clearly from Your Holy Spirit. Prepare my heart to be moved to follow Your prompting and let go of its stubbornness, devices, and preferences.

May the milk and honey of Your Word, Spirit, and life flow through me.

May the promise of the original purpose and potential of finding divine inspiration light me up now. May Your guidance be evident in my every brushstroke [or note or keystroke, etc.], in all my choices.

May You reveal to me what You wish to say and what I want to say in partnership and collaboration in this work.

May everyone who sees, hears, feels, or experiences this work and witnesses the process by which it is made feel Your joy and love for him or her personally and come to know more about You.

Protect me from temptations that would stunt or deter my growth as a son or daughter, artist, and person, and guide my every step to experiences, material, people, and places that would cause me to learn and grow.

May I be equipped to be as bold as You desire.

Please give me the energy I need to complete the project You give me to do.

I thank You for filling me with Your joy and pleasure in the process. I humble myself truly before You and worship You with all glory and honor and praise. Amen.

One prayer I did find comes from Julia Cameron's *The Artist's Way*.

An Artist's Prayer

O Great Creator,
We are gathered together in your name
That we may be of greater service to you
And to our fellows.
We offer ourselves to you as instruments.
We open ourselves to your creativity in our lives.
We surrender our old ideas.
We welcome your new and more expansive ideas.
We trust that you will lead us.
We trust that it is safe to follow you.
We know you created us and creativity
Is your nature and our own.
We ask you to unfold our lives
According in your plan, not our low self-worth.
Help us to believe that it is not too late

And that we are not too small or too flawed
To be healed—
By you and through each other—and made whole.
Help us to love one another,
To nurture each other's unfolding,
To encourage each other's growth,
And understand each other's fears.
Help us to know that we are not alone,
That we are loved and lovable.
Help us to create as an act of worship to you.[1]

Here is a prayer my friend Jeff Sparks sent to me. It comes from John Baillie's *A Diary of Private Prayer*:

O Holy Spirit, visit now this soul of mine, and tarry within it until eventide. Inspire all my thoughts. Pervade all my imaginations. Suggest all my decisions. Lodge in my will's most inward citadel and order all my doings. Be with me in my silence and in my speech, in my haste and in my leisure, in company and in solitude, in the freshness of the morning and in the weariness of the evening; and give me grace at all times to rejoice in thy mysterious companionship.[2]

Here is a Celtic blessing that touches on creativity very nicely:

May the light of your soul guide you.
May the light of your soul bless the work you do
With the secret love and warmth of your heart.
May you see in what you do the beauty of your own soul.
May the sacredness of your work bring healing, light, and renewal

To those who work with you and to those who see
and receive your work.
May your work never weary you.
May it release within you wellsprings of refreshment,
inspiration and excitement.
May you be present in what you do.
May you never become lost in the bland absences.
May the day never burden.
May the dawn find you awake and alert, approaching
your new day
With dreams, possibilities, and promises.
May evening find you gracious and fulfilled.
May you go into the night blessed, sheltered, and
protected.
May your soul calm, console, and renew you.

In *The Creative Call*, Janice Elsheimer makes the excellent suggestion that individual artists should write their own personal invitation to the Holy Spirit to come into their work and refer back to it often:

> The purpose of this prayer will be to call forth His creative, enlightening power whenever you begin to create, just as the classical writers did. The prayer should also remind you to offer yourself as a servant to the artist work God wants you to do. This will be your Artist's Prayer, which you can use to get started, to keep going, and to get past the inevitable blocks as you pursue your art.[3]

We've included a few blank pages in the back of this book to record your personal artist's prayer. Ask God to help you form the words so that they would express your heart toward Him. This will be a powerful tool in your journey toward finding divine inspiration.

CHAPTER 13

WISDOM FOR ARTISTS

I LOVE WISE QUOTES. Here are a few that God has led me to that might help in your journey of *Finding Divine Inspiration.*

ON YOUR UNIQUENESS AS A PERSON AND AN ARTIST

There is a vitality, a life force, an energy, a quick-ening, that is translated through you into action, and because there is only one of you in all time, this expression is unique. And if you block it, it will never exist through any other medium and will be lost.   —Martha Graham[1]

For we are God's workmanship, created in Christ Jesus to good works, which God prepared in advance for us to do (Ephesians 2:10).

It is within my power either to serve God or not to serve Him. Serving Him, I add to my own good and the good of the whole world. Not serving

Him, I forfeit my own good and deprive the world of that Good, which was in my power to create.

—Leo Tolstoy[2]

Our days are not extraordinary. They are filled with the mundane, with hassles mostly. And we? We are...a dime a dozen. Nothing special really. Probably a disappointment to God. But as C.S. Lewis wrote, "The value of...myth is that it takes all the things we know and restores to them the rich significance which has been hidden by 'the veil of familiarity.'" You are not what you think you are. There is a glory to your life that your Enemy fears, and he is hell-bent on destroying that glory before you act on it. This part of the answer will sound unbelieveable at first; perhaps it will sound too good to be true; certainly, you will wonder if it is true for you. But once you begin to see with those eyes, once you have begun to know it is true from the bottom of your heart, it will change everything. The story of your life is the story of the long and brutal assault on your heart by the one who knows what you could be and fears it.

—John Eldredge[3]

You saw me before I was born and scheduled each day of my life before I began to breathe. Every day was recorded in Your book (Ps. 139:16 TLB).

ON PERFECTIONISM

Perfectionism is a refusal to let yourself move ahead. It is a loop—an obsessive, debilitating closed system that causes you to get stuck in the details of what you are writing or painting or making and lose sight of the whole. "A painting is never finished. It simply stops in interesting places," said Paul Gardner. A book is never finished. But at a certain point you stop writing it and go on to the next thing. A film is never cut perfectly, but at a certain point you let go and call it done. That is a normal part of creativity—letting go. We always do the best that we can by the light we have to see by. —Julia Cameron[4]

Artists who seek perfection in everything are those who cannot attain it in anything.

—Eugene Delacroix[5]

Do not finish your work too much.

—Paul Gauguin[6]

ON HUMILITY

In a very real sense not one of us is qualified, but it seems that God continually chooses the most unqualified to do his work, to bear his glory. If we are qualified, we tend to think that we have done the job ourselves. If we are forced to accept our evident lack of qualification, then there's no danger that we will confuse God's work with our own, or God's glory with our own.

—Madeleine L'Engle[7]

Do you wish to be great? Then begin by being. Do you desire to construct vast and lofty fabric? Think first about the foundations of humility. The higher your structure is to be, the deeper must be its foundations.   —Augustine[8]

I know who I am. I know what I am. I know how evil I am, and I know how fallen I am. I think you've got to start there. I've had my days when I don't act to my convictions, but one area, if I could be proud of something of this band—that's sort of an oxymoron—it would be that each of the guys in the band are very humble people. I think it's a blessing. Here's my thing. I get out on stage and I know that there's probably fifty guys out there that could sing better than I could. But they're not there. But I don't know why I'm there. I believe I am a miracle. I believe that me up on stage singing is God having a joke, in a good way. Because God can do that, and He's so funny. God can take the foolish things and confound the wise, and I've become one of those people. That's what keeps us humble, the fact that we know who we are. We're very grateful. We *know* where it comes from…where these blessings come from, and whatever curve life throws us, we don't blame it on God. It's like A.W. Tozer said, "God is not winning, God is not losing, God is God. God is not success, God is not failure, God is God." Life didn't go smooth for Christ either. If you remember that, then you know who you are. All this is going to pass away; this is so temporary, what we do here. It may be fifteen, twenty years, twenty-five years, Lord willing. If we can keep making music, we may. But there are other things that count more for eternity.   Peter Furler[9]

Remember—the root word of *humble* and *human* is the same: *humus*; earth. We are dust. We are created; it is God who made us and not we ourselves. But we were made to be co-creators with our maker.   —Madeleine L'Engle[10]

IMAGINATION

Is your imagination stayed on God or is it starved? The starvation of the imagination is one of the most fruitful sources of exhaustion and sapping in a worker's life. If you have never used your imagination to put yourself before God, begin to do it now. It is no use waiting for God to come; you must put your imagination away from the face of idols and look unto Him and be saved. Imagination is the greatest gift God has given us and it ought to be devoted entirely to Him. If you have been bringing every thought into captivity to the obedience of Christ, it will be one of the greatest assets to faith when the time of trial comes, because your faith and the Spirit of God will work together.   —Oswald Chambers[11]

ON THE ROLE OF SKILL AND CRAFTSMANSHIP

I definitely feel like there is craft involved. You have to become a really good craftsman. You need to learn all the tools that are in the toolbox and learn to work with them; when to use them and how to use them. That's just your responsibility. If you've been given the gifts you have to learn how to use them and be good stewards of those gifts. You can be an extremely inspired person but if you don't know how to use the tools and you don't know how to put it down you're not going to get very far.   —Buzz McLauglin[12]

We get better and better at our work…. We get as skilled as we possibly can…so that when and if the Spirit comes in the right moment, we're at the typewriter.   —Walter Wangerin Jr.[13]

A work of art is the trace of a magnificent struggle.
—Robert Henri[14]

Let the student enter the school with this advice: No matter how good the school is, his education is in his own hands. All education must be self-education.   —Robert Henri[15]

One learns about painting by looking at and imitating other painters. I can't stress enough how important it is, if you are interested at all in painting, to look and to look a great deal at painting. There is no other way to find out about painting.
—Frank Stella[16]

ON FEAR

To win the war against fear, we must know the true God as He is revealed in the Bible. He works to give us lasting peace. He receives joy, not from condemning us but in rescuing us from the devil. Yes, the Lord will bring conviction to our hearts

concerning sin, but it is so He can deliver us from its power and consequence. In its place, the Lord works to establish healing, forgiveness and peace.
—Francis Frangipane[17]

Therefore, since we are surrounded by such a great cloud of witnesses, let us throw off everything that hinders and the sin that so easily entangles, and let us run with perseverance the race marked out for us (Hebrews 12:1).

Our deepest fear is not that we are inadequate. Our deepest fear is that we are powerful beyond measure. It is our light, not our darkness, that most frightens us. We ask ourselves, "Who am I to be brilliant, gorgeous, talented and fabulous?" Actually, who are you not to be? You are a child of God. Your playing small doesn't serve the world. There's nothing enlightened about shrinking so that other people won't feel secure around you. We were born to manifest the glory of God that is within us…. And as we let our own light shine, we unconsciously give other people permission to do the same. As we are liberated from our own fear, our presence automatically liberates other.
—Marianne Williamson[18]

The artist begins with a vision—a creative operation requiring an effort. Creativity takes courage.
—Henri Matisse[19]

Courage is fear that has said its prayers.
—Unknown[20]

CHAPTER 14

WRITER'S JOURNAL

THE NINE-YEAR PROCESS OF WRITING this book has been filled with highs and lows. There have been many wonderful affirmations and prophetic words and many frustrations and times when I thought about quitting. Through everything, the process of writing *Finding Divine Inspiration* has been a wonderful example of how collaboration with the Holy Spirit works. I've tried to do my part of gathering information and writing it down as God led me, often while fighting feelings of inadequacy. For His part, God not only gave the original idea, but He has also brought the promised inspiration and provided the material, opportunity, and strength to make it happen.

The following thoughts are taken from entries in my journal as God took me on this journey. In the interest of space and sanity, I've only included a few of the entries about the book from the dozens that were recorded. Looking back over these, I'm reminded how fragile and clueless I am and how patient and faithful He is.

THE JOURNAL

February 4, 1996: I had a drastic life change because of an unwanted separation and subsequent divorce. As a result, I gave up nearly all creative pursuits and desperately sought God for extended times nearly every day. During this time, I read Leanne Payne's *Listening Prayer*, started a daily journal on February 8, and began to learn to really wait and listen for God's voice.

Late 1996: Started praying and listening for God's direction before, during and after creative projects, and began to experience collaboration with the Holy Spirit in my work. It was an entirely new way of working.

Summer 1998: Experiences of collaborating with God in my creative process are really starting to accumulate, punctuated by the prayer-soaked process of producing Sky-Concert, the 30-minute fireworks-to-music show I produce for the radio station. God was present all through the project, and the finished show (with nearly three-quarters of a million people watching live and on TV) was a magnificent expression of God's joy!

September 10, 1998: The Vineyard arts group prayed for leading and waited to hear the Father's direction on what to paint for a special Advent service. It was the first time I saw the *Finding Divine Inspiration* principles working with a group, as God gave us unique ideas and direction when we invited Him into the process. During that time, in the Fall of 1998, I realized that this way of working and collaborating with God might be something I should write about. The accumulated thoughts were written down over a period of a few months starting in November 1998.

May 1999: I began interviewing well-known artists about the Holy Spirit's role their creative process, starting with author Walt Wangerin Jr. (*The Book of God*) and composer Randy Courts. The interviews were wonderful and showed me that different artists have different ways of working with God in the creative process.

June 1999: The only book I had read on Christianity and the arts was *How Shall We Then Live* by Francis Schaeffer. A friend at church mentioned that Madeleine L'Engle had written a book called *Walking on Water*, which became a wonderful resource for this book. God brought many other books and resources across my path, often in cool little supernatural ways. These were wonderful provisions that came after I prayed for God to guide my every step, in life and in the writing process.

October 19, 1999: Praying about the book, I journaled that I'd like it to be an important contribution to the world. I felt God said, "It is *Mine*, son. Don't be afraid; write it My way, son. I've given you what you need, now talk to the people you want."

September 1999: I was struggling with heavy spiritual attacks after writing sessions, feeling worthless, depressed, having crazy thoughts. This caused me to slowly become discouraged and back off from the project. One night I felt the Holy Spirit nudging me to turn on a Christian TV channel. The host was preaching about attacks from the enemy. His encouragement shined a light on the subtle lies I had bought into and caused me to realize that attacks were to be *expected* and that, in the power to God's Spirit, I should push through. I began asking some people to pray with me before I wrote.

Sometime later, as I was praying, I felt the Father saying I must see myself as a warrior, that I must walk into battle or be prepared to meet and vanquish the enemy and that I can't do it alone, and that I must work with other warriors. The realization came that I needed a regular prayer support team.

September 27, 1999: Praying about the book, I wrote, "…right now I feel this job is way too big for me and I don't know anything…Lord, should I pursue a publisher? I feel you saying no until I get some interviews with artists. Lord, I don't want to worry about that, but leave it in your hands. Stepping out is not comfortable, but difficult and I feel like I want to retreat and be invisible, to be comfy and romanticize this and not venture out."

January 15, 2000: Another artist recommended that I visit the Billy Graham Center Museum in Wheaton, Illinois, saying it is a treasure trove of Christian Contemporary art. In praying about going, I wrote that I felt God saying, "Don't go to Wheaton as the focal point, but as a little pilgrimage. The focal point is *Me* working with you and in you now… I'm not ready for you to be published yet, son."

January 25, 2000: Home group prayed for me on a Tuesday night, after I had fasted Monday and part of Tuesday. The prayers and words were wonderful and anointed and an incredible way to be commissioned and confirmed before the trip to Wheaton. The experience once again brought the importance of community to my attention, insights that later became chapter 10 "A Future for the Arts." I had taken the week off to write and go to Wheaton and received some neat revelations during that time.

January 28, 2000: The Billy Graham Museum held many, many blessings, confirmations, and information. The curator let me look through all the catalogues of their archives, possibly the best collection of Christian art in the United States. I spent hours there, listening to the Holy Spirit about artists who I should get in touch with. I got several names and contacts, including Ron Dicianni, who I called a couple of weeks later. Ron's featured exhibit at the museum clearly showed that the Holy Spirit is guiding his work.

January 29, 2000: Recapping the events of the past few days, I wrote, "I've prayed about and dedicated every interview and every time I've written anything. Fasted and prayed on Monday (the 24th), got some direction for an opening for the book." As I worked on the book during that time, God gave me wonderful thoughts about Adam's collaboration with Him in the garden. Those thoughts turned into Chapter 2, "Divine Collaboration."

February 2, 2000: Praying at lunch during work, I felt God saying, "I want you and I love you, son. I enjoy what you are doing, but I want to know you, Scott." Just more affirmation that, as Oswald Chambers often says, it's not about the work you do for God, it's about the relationship.

February 4, 2000: I was able to interview Ron DiCianni and it went very well. He is very surrendered to true collaboration with the Holy Spirit. I felt a renewed purpose and enthusiasm afterward. He recommended I talk to (painter) Thomas Blackshear, which turned out to be another wonderful interview.

February 12, 2000: In my quiet time, God showed me in Psalm 22 that David wrote prophetic words in an artistic way. He was a prophetic artist! This was put into the book in Chapter 4, "The Art of the Bible."

March 11, 2000: On a retreat day, I got some insight about collaboration while in prayer and study. I found out later that my friend Jeff Sparks—one of my prayer supporters—had prayed for just that, that day. The insight was about the nature of artists as listeners, and it became the foundation for Chapter 3, "The Work of the Artist."

March 23, 2000: I wrote a page and a half in the book on Romans 12:1-2, which caught my eye when one of the Newsboys wrote it on my daughter's concert shirt after the Peter Furler interview. This went into Chapter 6, "Developing a Listening Lifestyle," and was a wonderful addition. It was more unique provision.

May 1, 2000: I wrote in my journal, "I feel I should write down the path You've taken me on in the process of writing this book." As a result, this chapter was born. I started taking these thoughts from my journals and adding them in.

May 27, 2000: I wrote, "A month or so ago in talking to Eric Poland (Producer/Director) about specific examples of being guided by the Holy Spirit, I was reminded of a story that Gary Bayer (Actor/Director), our mutual friend, had told us. Immediately I felt You were confirming that I needed to interview Gary for the book. Now, in New Harmony, I will do that. This morning I decided to walk down to the house Gary is staying in to set up a time. It was maybe a three-block walk, and I felt You saying gently I should go. As I passed a landmark (the roofless church) I thought about going in for a moment, but felt You encouraging to 'walk on.' Nearing the house, I saw Gary come out and get into his car, and he was just putting it in gear as I walked up. He was heading to his mother's and would be gone for a while. Perfect timing. We set up a time, and he was excited." As I've tried to hear Him, God has led me on many walks that turn out to be just the right timing. It's a very sweet thing.

July 19, 2000: Felt You said to me, "Finish the book, the book, the book. I'm not working through you when you're not writing, son. Don't be scared. Write when I say." God is so merciful to nudge us along when we need it. His patience with us is astounding.

February 20, 2000: I wrote, "They prayed for me at home group again tonight. Someone felt the book is a ministry, and they were excited about it. Another person felt that the frustration I might be feeling with the length of time its taking is part of the process of You showing me things that I need to know, that I would hear from You and other people." That turned out to be exactly right.

May 10, 2001: After a lot of prayer and seeking, I felt God's direction to start an artist home group with a fellow artist, Tony Spitler. It was a real encouragement, serving as a haven and training ground for several of us.

August 18, 2001: Praying on a Saturday, I journaled about the creative process, the importance of overcoming fear and doubt. Julia Cameron talks about this eloquently in *The Artist's Way*. I wrote that You were saying to me, "Artistic endeavor isn't neat, but sloppy and earthy, stinky and truly appalling to some, son." Interesting.

September 2001: After the shock of 9/11 faded, I had renewed focus and energy to complete the book. It was time to see the arts renewed for God!

September 22, 2001: I wrote that I believed God was saying, "No one has all the answers on this subject. The work of the Holy Spirit remains a mystery." This is good to remember and should keep me open-minded!

December 12, 2001: Thanking the Lord for answered prayer after a successful Advent service, I wrote, "We coated this Advent in prayer again and received great response. The church secretary said the message at the service (about *choosing* joy) was perfect. It just felt like a revelation while it was being given, and she said in her spirit, 'That's it! That's what it's all about!' *You* brought it, and I humble myself." Later I wrote, "Reading Oswald yesterday… 'Any problem that comes while I obey God (and there will be many) increases my overjoyed delight, because I know that my Father knows and cares, and I can watch and anticipate how He will unravel my problems.' That's true and part of what I've learned through this Advent process. You've moved to work out all kinds of problems and struggles in the process. It was wonderful to watch."

February 19, 2002: I wrote, "As I've geared up to write during a week's vacation, I typed up and emailed support letters to people in my church community. Experienced some sense of being overwhelmed as I started today, of being inadequate, but understand that is satan's lie, his attempt at keeping me in fear. I found out the book and I had been brought up at a prayer meeting the Friday before, that the prayer time had shifted toward the arts and artists and that intercession was done on our behalf. No one there knew that I was getting ready to write this week. It's a confirmation. One of so many."

November 2004: I wrote, "Submitting the book to publishers and waiting to hear back. Assistant Pastor Randy Gooder spoke at the morning service on asking God about one courageous act He might have you do. I had something in mind that I thought would come up when we quieted ourselves for a moment and listened, but to my surprise, what I heard was, 'Do the seminars.' Seminars about *Finding Divine Inspiration!*"

January 2005: I wrote, "The synopsis for the book was posted on the Writer's Edge website on Monday the third and I got a phone call from a publisher who was (very excited) about the idea behind the book. Said she had been speaking and preaching about this. Wanted to thank me for being obedient to the Holy Spirit!" We didn't end up publishing with her, but the confirmation was very encouraging.

March 8, 2005: We did the first *Finding Divine Inspiration* Seminar at the Vineyard on Saturday, March 5, and it was a beautiful experience. I spent a few weeks beforehand condensing the material of the book into seminar form, and it translated very well. About 35 people attended the five-hour seminar, and it was just a joy. I wrote in my journal, "More encouraged by the seminar now that it's setting in. Several good comments from people about how they loved it. Lord, this confirmation of what you've been doing in me is amazing! I'm surprised, I guess, Lord, that so much seemed to resonate with them and that you moved so wonderfully." I had expected that there would be points in the material that I'd need to refine after the seminar was over, but almost all of it seemed to work! This was an affirmation that I was on the right track and nearing the end of the writing process. Thank you, Lord!

March 26, 2007 After trying to find an agent to represent the book and receiving everything from no response to rude one-line answers to helpful and courteous letters, I decided, after a lot of prayer, to contact publishers on my own. I chose several that looked interesting from the *Christian Writer's Market Guide*, and went to Borders one night to see how many of their books I could find on the shelves. I was impressed with Destiny Image, both with the subjects they publish and the philosophy they have.

July 2007: After praying about it, I sent a proposal in to Destiny Image in March and then contacted them in July. The Acquisitions Editor, Ronda, was very enthusiastic, and we began talking about preparing the book to go through the evaluation process. This really seemed right!

October 13, 2007: I've spent the last month finishing the book, adding around one hundred pages. The prayer support team has faithfully prayed for the process during this time, and the effects were really wonderful. My prayer and writing time has been supernaturally fruitful, and I've been very aware of God's presence. I finished the manuscript and sent it to Ronda four minutes before midnight on the fourteenth, the day of my 45th birthday. God's timing is such a wonderful gift!

THE FIRST STEP TO DIVINE INSPIRATION

HAVE YOU EVER FELT A SENSE that you are being gently nudged, mysteriously urged—almost guided—to step toward something that has not fully material- ized in your mind? It's more of a feeling or an impression, and you experience a tinge of excitement and romanticism as you think about the possibilities. Could it be a new start is coming? Maybe it's a new love relationship or personal healing or a new way of thinking about things.

What if it's not some accomplishment or state of being that is calling you, but some One. Someone who knows all about you, every detail, even things you can't remember, and loves you completely as you are.

What if this Someone is calling you to your true, authentic place in the world... not only the seen, material, earthly world, but also the transcendent, infinite, spiritual, eternal world? The truth is that you have a unique, desig- nated place in both realms, and there is only one Guide and

Lover who can lead you into that place. Jesus wants to collaborate with you to bring everything you were meant to be into its rightful place. It's a journey that may not be fully completed in the lifetime you have on earth, and it will be fraught with struggles and setbacks, but it is the truest and most rewarding way to live.

To join God in the path of collaboration that has been designed especially for you—before you were even a thought in your parents' minds—invite Him to live inside your heart. Tell Him you want to put your life in His hands, to become His friend and do His will on earth. The One who is calling you out is just a moment in time away. He is waiting patiently with open arms and an accepting smile.

This is the new start you've been dreaming about, and in it are love, healing, and a fulfilling new life. If you've decided to start on this journey of becoming friends with God, e-mail us at start@FindingDivineInspiration.com, and we'll help you find a church in your community where you can grow, learn, and find love.

ENDNOTES

PREFACE

1. Daniel Pink, *A Whole New Mind* (New York: Berkley Publishing Group, 2005), Introduction.

CHAPTER 1: A NEW RENAISSANCE

1. Harriet Beecher Stowe, *Uncle Tom's Cabin*, (New York: Barnes & Noble Classics, 2003), taken from the beginning supplement titled, "The World of Harriet Beecher Stowe and Uncle Tom's Cabin," xi.

2. "Gibson's Way With Words," *USA Today*, July 31, 2006, http://www.usatoday.com/life/people/2006-07-31-gibson-remarks_x.htm (accessed 12 August 2008).

3. Tim Ryan, "Embodying Christ," *Starbulletin.com*, February 22, 2004, http://starbulletin.com/2004/02/22/features/story1.html (accessed 12 August 2008).

4. Bob Briner, *Roaring Lambs* (Grand Rapids, MI: Zondervan, 1993), 139.

5. *Ibid*, 28.

CHAPTER 2: DIVINE COLLABORATION

1. Stella Terrill Mann, quoted in Julia Cameron, *The Artist's Way: A Spiritual Path to Higher Creativity* (New York: J.P. Tarcher/Putnam, 2002), 49.

2. Francis Bacon, quoted in Francis Schaeffer, *Art in the Bible*, (Downers Grove, IL: InterVarsity Press, 1973), 10.

3. A paraphrase of Rainer Maria Rilke, quoted in Hans-Georg Gadamer, *Truth and Method* (New York: Continuum, 1999), quoted in Kurt M. Denk, *Making Connections, Finding Meaning, Engaging the World: Theory and Techniques for Ignatian Reflection on Service for and with Others*, http://www.loyola.edu/Justice/documents/Template_for_Ignation_Reflection.doc (accessed 12 August 2008), 18.

4. Madeleine L'Engle, *Walking on Water* (New York: Harold Shaw Publishers, 1998), 92.

CHAPTER 3: THE WORK OF THE ARTIST

1. Malcolm Muggeridge, quoted in *Brainy Quote*, http://www.brainyquote.com/quotes/quotes/m/malcolmmug162600.html (accessed 12 August 2008).

2. Steve Turner, Imagine: *A Vision for Christians in the Arts* (Downers Grove, IL: InterVarsity Press, 2000), 88.

3. Madeleine L'Engle, *Walking On Water*, 20.

4. Dallas Willard, *Hearing God*, 17.

5. Plato, quoted in *Thinkexist.com*, http://thinkexist.com/quotation/music_and_rhythm_find_their_way_into_the_secret/158901.html (accessed 12 August 2008).

6. Attributed to Leanne Payne; no reference available.

7. Steve Turner, *Imagine*, 61.

8. Josef Peiper, *Only the Lover Sings* (Ft. Collins, CO: Ignatius Press, 1990), 72-73.

9. Pablo Picasso, quoted in Clint Brown, *Artist to Artist* (Corvallis, OR: Jackson Creek Press, 1998), 147.

10. Kurt Vonnegut and Lee Stringer, *Like Shaking Hands with God* (New York: Seven Stories Press, 1999), 47.

11. Bono, quoted in Edna Gundersen, "U2: Rock Giants Leave '90s Behind to Break Out of Zoo of Pop, Rap," *USA Today*, October 30, 2000, Life section, 2D.

12. Madeleine L'Engle, *Walking on Water*, 19.

13. *Ibid*, 27.

14. Johannes Brahms, quoted in Patrick Kavanaugh, *Spiritual Lives of the Great Composers* (Grand Rapids, MI: Zondervan, 1992), 146.

15. Dallas Willard, *Hearing God*, 212.

16. Diane Apostolos-Cappadona and Lucinda Ebersole, *Women, Creativity and the Arts* (New York: Continuum, 1995), 1-2.

17. Dallas Willard, *Hearing God*, 151.

18. Gilles Neret, *Michelangelo* (Koln, Germany: Taschen, 2005), 83.

19. Michelangelo, quoted in C. Ryan, *The Poetry of Michelangelo: An Introduction* (Madison, NJ: Fairleigh Dickinson University Press, 1998), 208.

20. Steve Turner, *Imagine*, 22.

Chapter 4: The Art of the Bible

1. Pablo Picasso, quoted in *Thinkexist.com*, http://thinkexist.com/quotation/god_is_really_only_another_artist_he_invented_the/143227.html (accessed 12 August 2008).

2. Francis Schaeffer, *Art and the Bible*, 15.

3. J.S. Bach, quoted in Patrick Kavanaugh, *Spiritual Lives of the Great Composers*, 22.

4. Steve Turner, *Imagine*, 70-71.

Chapter 5: Historical Examples of Divine Inspiration

1. Patrick Kavanaugh, *Spiritual Lives of the Great Composers*, 30.

2. *Ibid*, 31-32.

3. Robert Manson Myers, *Handel's Messiah, a Touchstone of Taste* (New York: Octagon Books, 1971), 80.

4. Leanne Payne, *Listening Prayer* (Grand Rapids, MI: Baker Books, 1994), 23.

5. Richard Wagner, quoted in Patrick Kavanaugh, *Spiritual Lives of the Great Composers*, 23.

6. Johannes Brahms, quoted in *Ibid*, 146.

7. Antonin Dvorak, quoted in *Ibid*, 152.

8. Franz Joseph Haydn, quoted in *Ibid*, 42.

9. Noel B. Gerson, *Harriet Beecher Stowe: A Biography* (Westport, CT: Praeger Publishers, 1976), 65.

10. Harriet Beecher Stowe, quoted in Charles Edward Stowe, *The Life of Harriet Beecher Stowe: Compiled From Her Letters and Journals* (New York: Houghton Mifflin, 1890), 157.

11. Jim Tomberlin, sermon, (Colorado Springs, CO: Woodman Valley Chapel, April 2000). Also referenced at WACRAL.org/page19.html and published in *Our Daily Bread* in 2000, which referenced Tim Hansel, *Eating Problems for Breakfast* (Nashville, TN: Word Publishing, 1988), 33-34.

12. A letter from Samuel F.B. Morse to his brother Sydney on May 31, 1844, in the Library of Congress.

13,14,15. Ann Lamont, *21 Great Scientists Who Believed the Bible* (Brisbane, Australia: Creation Science Foundation, 1995), 22, quoted in K. Graham, L. Hicks,

D. Shimmin, and G. Thompson, *Biology: God's Living Creation* (Pensacola, FL: A Beka Books, 1986), 63.

16. Giorgio Vasari, *The Lives of the Artists* (Oxford: Oxford University Press, 1998, originally published 1549), 177.

17. Volker Gebhardt, *The History of Art* (Hauppage, New York: Barron's, 1998), 36-37.

18. Giorgio Vasari, *The Lives of the Artists*, 176.

19. *Ibid*, 177.

20. Bob Briner, *Roaring Lambs*, 46.

Chapter 6: Developing a Listening Lifestyle

1. Dwight L. Moody, *What Think Ye of Christ?*, sermon (England, 1973-1975), available at *Bartleby.com*, http://www.bartleby.com/268/10/10.html (accessed 12 August 2008).

2. Walter Wangerin Jr., *Whole Prayer* (Grand Rapids, MI: Zondervan, 2001).

3. Madeleine L'Engle, *Walking on Water*, 139.

4. Oswald Chambers, *My Utmost for His Highest* (Grand Rapids, MI: Discovery House, 1992), December 9.

5. *Ibid*, March 21.

6. *Ibid*, June 13.

7. Betsy Walker, sermon (Indianapolis, IN: Vineyard Community Church, October 2007), www.betsywalker.com.

8. Dallas Willard, *Hearing God*, 152.

9. Madeleine L'Engle, *Walking on Water*, 156.

10. *Ibid*, 84.

11. Julia Cameron, *The Artist's Way*, 12.

12. Leanne Payne, *Listening Prayer*, 74.

13. *Ibid*, 74.

14. *Ibid*, 75.

15. *Ibid*.

CHAPTER 7: HINDRANCES TO HEARING

1. Steve Turner, *Imagine*, 42.

2. Julia Cameron, *The Artist's Way*, 87.

3. Dallas Willard, *Hearing God*, 38.

4. Madeleine L'Engle, *Walking on Water*, 53.

5. Leanne Payne, *Listening Prayer*, 158-159.

6. Louis B. Smedes, *Sex for Christians* (Grand Rapids, MI: Eerdmans, 1976), 109-110.

7. Mark Joseph, *Rock and Roll Rebellion* (New York: Broadman & Holman Publishers, 1999), 278-279.

8. Dallas Willard, *Hearing God*, 88.

9. Steve Turner, *Imagine*, 119.

10. Leanne Payne, *Listening Prayer*, 132.

CHAPTER 8: PERSONAL EXAMPLES OF TRUE COLLABORATIONS

1. Madeleine L'Engle, *Walking on Water*, 22.

2. Robert E. Webber, Ed., *Music and the Arts in Christian Worship: Book Two* (Nashville, TN: Star Song, 1994).

CHAPTER 10: A FUTURE FOR THE ARTS

1. Steve Turner, *Imagine*, 121.

2. Jack Clemo, quoted in *Ibid*, 122.

3. Gary Bayer, interview with the author, May 27, 2000.

4. Dan Haseltine, interview with the author.

5. Madeleine L'Engle, *Walking on Water*, 219.

CHAPTER 11: Q & A ABOUT COLLABORATING WITH GOD IN YOUR CREATIVE PROCESS

1. Leanne Payne, *Listening Prayer*, 136-137.

2. *Ibid*.

3. Dallas Willard, *Hearing God*, 56.

4. Dr. Henry Cloud and Dr. John Townsend, *Boundaries: When to Say YES, When to say NO, To Take Control of Your Life* (Grand Rapids, MI: Zondervan, 1992), 99-100.

CHAPTER 12: PRAYERS FOR CREATIVITY AND INSPIRATION

1. Julia Cameron, *The Artist's Way*, 211.

2. John Baillie, *A Diary of Private Prayer* (New York: Fireside, 1949).

3. Janice Elsheimer, *The Creative Call* (New York: Shaw Publishing, 2001), 72.

CHAPTER 13: WISDOM FOR ARTISTS

1. Martha Graham, quoted in Julia Cameron, *The Artist's Way*, 75.

2. Leo Tolstoy, quoted in *Mission Moment*, March 4, 2002, http://www.missionmoment.org/allmissionmoments.htm (accessed 12 August 2008).

3. John Eldredge, *Waking the Dead: The Glory of a Heart Fully Alive* (Nashville, TN: Thomas Nelson Publishers, 2003), 33.

4. Julia Cameron, *The Artist's Way*, 119-120.

5. Eugene Delacroix, quoted in Clint Brown, *Artist to Artist*, 182.

6. Paul Gaugin, quoted in "Paul Gauguin - French Artist From Art History," *The Art World*, http://www.the-art-world.com/history/gauguin.htm (accessed 12 August 2008).

7. Madeleine L'Engle, *Walking on Water*, 70.

8. Augustine, quoted in "Saint Augustine Quotes," *Brainy Quote*, http://www.brainyquote.com/quotes/authors/s/saint_augustine.html (accessed 12 August 2008).

9. Peter Furler, in an interview with the author, April 2000.

10. Madeleine L'Engle, *Walking on Water*, 154.

11. Oswald Chambers, *My Utmost for His Highest*, February 11.

12. Buzz McLaughlin, telephone conversation with the author, May 2002.

13. Walter Wangerin Jr., in discussion with author, May 1999.

14. Robert Henri, quoted in Clint Brown, *Artist to Artist*, 12.

15. *Ibid*, 85.

16. Frank Stella, quoted in *Ibid*, 88.

17. Francis Frangipane, quoted in "To win the war against fear," *Great Quotes for Quoting: Quotes for Pastors, Teachers, and Writers*, http://thequotes.wordpress.com/2007/07/19/to-win-the-war-against-fear/ (accessed 12 August 2008).

18. Marianne Williamson, *A Return to Love* (New York: HarperCollins, 1992), 190.

19. Henri Matisse, quoted in Clint Brown, *Artist to Artist*, 62.

20. Quoted in J. John and Mark Stibbe, *A Box of Delights* (Grand Rapids, MI: Kregel Publishers, 2002), 6.

SUGGESTED READING

Briner, Bob. *Roaring Lambs*. Grand Rapids, MI: Zondervan, 1993.

Cameron, Julia. *The Artist's Way: A Spiritual Path to Higher Creativity*. New York: J.P. Tarcher/Putnam, 2002. (This is not a Christian book, but it is highly spiritual and helpful. The new age philosophies are easily sifted out.)

Cloud, Dr. Henry, and Dr. John Townsend. *Boundaries: When to Say YES, When to say NO, To Take Control of Your Life*. Grand Rapids, MI: Zondervan, 1992.

Cook, Marshall J. *Freeing Your Creativity*. Cincinnati, OH: Writer's Digest Books, 1992.

Eldredge, John. *Waking the Dead: The Glory of a Heart Fully Alive*. Nashville, TN: Thomas Nelson Publishers, 2003.

Elsheimer, Janice. *The Creative Call*. New York: Shaw Publishing, 2001.

Henri, Robert. *The Art Spirit.* Boulder, CO: Icon Editions, 1923.

L'Engle, Madeleine. *Walking on Water.* New York: Harold Shaw Publishers, 1980, 1998.

Noland, Rory. *The Heart of the Artist.* Grand Rapids, MI: Zondervan, 1999.

Payne, Leanne. *Listening Prayer.* Grand Rapids, MI: Baker Books, 1994.

Schaeffer, Francis. *Art and the Bible.* Downers Grove, IL: InterVarsity Press, 1973.

Schaeffer, Francis. *How Shall We Then Live?* New York: Harper Collins Distribution Services, 1980.

Turner, Steve. *Imagine: A Vision for Christians in the Arts.* Downers Grove, IL: InterVarsity Press, 2000.

Willard, Dallas. *Hearing God.* Downers Grove, IL: InterVarsity Press, 1999.

Willard, Dallas. *The Divine Conspiracy.* New York: HarperCollins, 1998.

My Artist's Prayer

Author Contact Information

To contact Scott for professional voiceover work, go to:
www.JScottMcElroy.com.

For information on scheduling a Finding Divine Inspiration
seminar and artist event go to:
www. FindingDivineInspiration.com

Additional copies of this book and other book titles from DESTINY IMAGE are available at your local bookstore.

Call toll-free: 1-800-722-6774.

Send a request for a catalog to:

Destiny Image® Publishers, Inc.

P.O. Box 310

Shippensburg, PA 17257-0310

"Speaking to the Purposes of God for This Generation and for the Generations to Come."

**For a complete list of our titles,
visit us at www.destinyimage.com.**